2-21-75

VAN NOSTRAND REINHOLD MANUALS

GENERAL EDITOR: W.S. TAYLOR

Pottery and Ceramics

David Hamilton

Van Nostrand Reinhold
Manual of Pottery and
Ceramics

VNR VAN NOSTRAND REINHOLD COMPANY
New York   Cincinnati

Acknowledgments are made to the following for permission to reproduce the illustrations on the pages shown:

Ashmolean Museum, Oxford, 113 (top), 142; K. Barton, 153; British Museum, London, 12, 14, 57, 58, 100 (bottom), 102 (right and bottom), 108, 111 (bottom), 135, 173; Count Cesare Cicogna, 99; P. A. Clayton, 17; German Archaeological Institute, Rome, 15; Gulbenkian Museum, Durham, 28; Kansas Gallery of Art, 61; Los Angeles County Museum of Art, 74; the Louvre, Paris, 100 (top); Ministry of Works, 111 (top); Musées Royaux d'Art et d'Histoire, Brussels, 12; Objects USA: The Johnson Collection of Contemporary Crafts, 19, 79 (top), 151; Miss J. Poncelet, 126 (top); Portsmouth City Art Gallery, 63, 66, 110 (bottom), 113 (bottom), 120, 152 (bottom); Royal Scottish Museum, Edinburgh, 102 (top); Irene Sims, 79 (bottom); Edwin Smith, 14, 57, 111 (top); P. Smith, 73 (bottom); Southampton City Art Gallery, 109 (bottom), 125, 126, 127 (bottom), 145; Jeff Teasdale, 29; Victoria and Albert Museum, London, 18, 122, 172; M. Walchowa, 152 (top).

Van Nostrand Reinhold Company
Regional Offices: New York
Cincinnati Chicago Millbrae
Dallas

Van Nostrand Reinhold Company
International Offices:
London Toronto Melbourne

Copyright © 1974 by Thames and
Hudson Ltd, London
Library of Congress Catalog Card
Number 73-19428
ISBN 0-442-23086-9

Printed in Great Britain by
Jarrold and Sons Ltd, Norwich

Published in the U.S.A. in 1974 by
Van Nostrand Reinhold Company
A Division of Litton Educational
Publishing, Inc. 450 West 33rd
Street, New York N.Y. 10001

16 15 14 13 12 11 10 9 8 7 6 5 4 3 2 1

Contents

Acknowledgments

I wish to thank the Directors of Portsmouth City Museum and Art Gallery and Southampton City Art Gallery for permission to reproduce work from their collections, Lee Nordness for his assistance in providing illustrations from the Exhibition 'Objects USA', the Los Angeles Museum and Art Gallery for providing the illustration of the work of John Mason (page 74). The staff and students of the Ceramics Workshop of Portsmouth Polytechnic were very patient and helpful when we were photographing workshop equipment and processes; my thanks to all of them.

David Ash gave his time and skill most generously in photographing all the workshop illustrations, and many of the finished objects, and Mrs R. Rogers pioneered her way through my notes to produce a typescript; to them both I am profoundly grateful, as I am to Gerry Tucker who provided the line-drawings, and Dr B. Daley for his comments on Chapter 2.

This book is dedicated to the late Bruce Adams, as an acknowledgment of the friendship and advice he unselfishly gave to all of us who were his students and friends.

D. H.

Introduction

The aim of this book is to introduce the processes and techniques of ceramics. It is not my intention to discuss philosophies or principles of art and design, although these may be generated by working in the medium. Not all students assimilate information at the same rate; a manual is a reference source, particularly for those students who find it difficult to understand and absorb all they have seen or been told. The change from subject-orientated to student-orientated art education tends to militate against systematic teaching. Written and illustrated texts may facilitate a more flexible studio teaching method.

After a short history of the art, the form of the book follows that of the ceramic process itself, starting with the basic materials and how they may be formed, and ending with final surface treatments. Such theory as is included will be found where it is necessary to the clear understanding of the process. Equipment is described at appropriate and relevant points, so that the options at any one time may be considered against the available tools. The only exception to this is the chapter on kilns, which pre-empts any discussion of what can be done because the kiln size and type will determine what is possible.

While a fuller understanding of the science of glazes would be gained from a more theoretical approach than I have chosen, it is my experience that first-year students do not respond readily to such teaching. It has been my practice for some years to provide basic recipes, or limit recipes, and for each student to introduce one variable at a time (e.g. the addition of another mineral or changing the firing temperature), so that experience is gradually assimilated; at some point early in the second year a series of discussions of the chemical and physical aspects of glazes is of much greater significance.

It would be presumptuous to pretend that the information contained here will prove sufficient for all students throughout their working lives; I have tried to lay the foundations for a practical first-year full-time course. No two teachers would agree on the precise form or content of such a foundation, and it is inevitable that the content and layout illustrate my own understanding of what a student might need.

I would not wish to interfere with the enthusiasm of a teacher working in a studio. But there are a number of

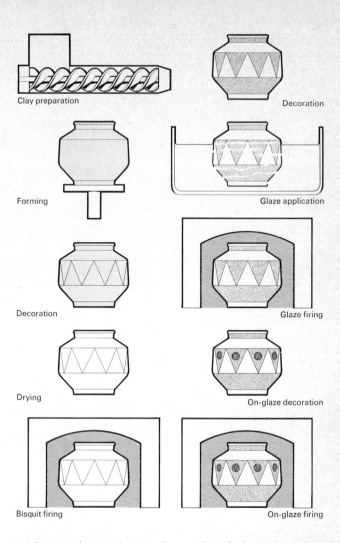

Clay preparation

Decoration

Forming

Glaze application

Decoration

Glaze firing

Drying

On-glaze decoration

Bisquit firing

On-glaze firing

The stages in the ceramic manufacturing process.

teachers and part-time students who, finding themselves in a new studio, or given new responsibilities, are overwhelmed by the variety of equipment and materials which they may inherit. For those who have not had the benefit of a full-time ceramics course, this book may help to solve some of the mysteries of ceramic art. It should be remembered that the art of ceramics is very old, and techniques and skills were accumulated only by practical experience.

Most towns and cities have art galleries or museums with ceramic collections, and these can be a constant source of ideas and information.

The importance of carefully recording one's results cannot be over-stressed. It may seem time-consuming at first, but nothing can be more frustrating than to obtain a fine colour or texture and have little or no idea how it was achieved.

Finally, one piece of philosophy. Skill and technique have no virtue in themselves: they are a means to an end.

I have never seen a poorly made, exciting ceramic object, but I have seen a good deal of dull but well-made ceramics (both hand- and factory-made). By teaching skills we are attempting to educate the senses to a heightened awareness. Craftsmanship has come to be identified with 'making' skills at the expense of imagination. Ceramics is a craft-based art but the balance between craft and art must be maintained.

'The moving force for the artist is the creative impulse, and the material serves to make that impulse reality'—Paul Klee.

Egyptian red polished clay vessel with
white decoration, *c.* 3500 B C.

1 The development of ceramics

Because of the nature of the ceramic process, which demands a permanent site and a stable environment in order to flourish, the earliest known examples of ceramic art are from those areas of the world which were the first to develop a stable agrarian society. The earliest known objects, *c.* 10,000 BC, are small models of figures, probably used in religious or magical ceremonies. As clay was plentiful, it was soon found that heat would make the clay more durable and that enough heat would render the clay rock-hard. The development of hollow forms, for storage or cooking, came later. Throughout history clay has been shaped into forms which were familiar to the maker and so we find that the earliest forms resemble fruit, baskets or stone containers. With the invention of the techniques of metal-forming, cheap clay imitations found a ready market. This phenomenon of the use of clay to reproduce other materials recurs frequently throughout history.

As Egypt and the Near East were the first parts of the world to develop an identifiable social pattern it is from this area that the earliest known ceramics came. Coloured pottery was being produced as early as the fifth millennium BC. Kilns rather than open fires have been found, and indeed would be essential to permit the manufacture of high-quality work. While some sort of wheel would have been used to help in the rounding of clay forms, the use of the wheel for thrown forms is usually attributed to Egypt in about 2000 BC. About this time the first glazes were used. Until this time burnishing of the surface was the only known method of decreasing the porosity of fired clay. Alkaline glazes were in common use and fritted lead glazes were developed. All the wares were relatively low-fired and most of the glazes were fired at so low a temperature that they have worn away, leaving us only a vague approximation of the initial richness of the fired piece. Alongside the skills of pot-making developed brick and tile manufacture and decoration. Unfired clay strengthened with straw was normally used but in large public buildings, in Assyria in particular, modelled and fired bricks were favoured for their permanence and grandeur.

This increase in technical skills led to the production of ceramics and pottery in such quantities that they could be traded with neighbouring countries. New techniques and

Kylix from Knossos (Late Minoan
III, c. 1200 BC), known as the
Octopus Goblet. The form is thrown,
with painted design, and unglazed.

forms rapidly spread to all areas of the known world.
Trading contacts reached as far as China, which is known to
have a tradition of ceramics dating as far back as 2000 or
3000 BC. A particular influence on Chinese ceramics was the
discovery of the techniques of bronze-casting, which
encouraged a style of pottery similar in form to that of cast
metal. Of greater significance was the development of the
techniques of high-fired ceramics, which dates from the
third or fourth centuries BC.

Although Europe was producing pottery two or three
thousand years before the birth of Christ it is in the Mediter-
ranean islands and those countries with overland and sea
trading routes with the Near East that the art developed to
the greatest degree. In Crete, 1500–1000 BC, the forms
produced were primarily useful but they illustrate a quality
and style of decoration that was developed by the Greeks
700–300 BC to produce the forms of classical antiquity.
These sophisticated forms owe little to the natural quality
of clay, being turned to conform to an aesthetic ideal rather
than an expression of the material. Most of these objects
were made for ceremonial use, and a simpler form of ware
was in daily use. The material used to produce these superb
illustrations of gods and classical myths is called *terra
sigillata* (see page 112) and they are particularly valued as the

Greek vase: a thrown and turned form with images painted in coloured clay, unglazed.

major source of information about the style and quality of Greek painting of the period.

With the establishment of Rome as a political and imperial power the ideologies and philosophies of Greece spread throughout Europe as far as the Scottish border. Until this time the techniques and forms had been much the same as in any other simple agrarian society. From the moment of conquest the ware was transformed in style and technical quality into that considered acceptable by the forces of occupation. What is so remarkable is that, regardless of the country where the ware was made, the same skill and type of result was achieved. Of particular importance is the relief decoration in imitation of metal-moulding techniques. Little of the ware is glazed although both glass and glaze techniques were known. As the Roman influence declined, so the whole of Europe returned to a state of near chaos and the momentum which the Romans had injected into European ceramics was lost. The forms, techniques and skills were superseded by more barbaric influences. While the quality of form remained vital there was little technical innovation; most of the ware was simply thrown, with engobe decoration and the occasional use of a waterproof lead glaze, particularly on the interior of the form.

Arretine-ware bowl made in Tuscany between 30 BC and AD 40. The original flared base on which it stood is missing.

While the Roman Empire waxed and waned, in China ceramics continued to develop. It is likely that the use of lead as a low-temperature glaze was imported from the West, but the development of high-fired stonewares about 300 BC, and white porcelain in the ninth century AD, was to dominate the world of ceramics for nearly a thousand years.

In common with many other societies, the Chinese buried ceramic vessels and models with their dead. The figures and animals which date from the T'ang period (AD 618–906) are particularly fine examples. The Sung period (960–1279) is renowned for the excellence of the ceramics produced, which illustrate highly developed skills and techniques.

Only with the establishment of Islam (ninth century AD) in the Near East was there any progress comparable to the achievements of the Chinese potters. Trade between the Islamic countries and China was regular, as would be natural between the two most powerful empires of Asia. The Persians exported their copper-blue wares and imported Chinese porcelain. In an attempt to reproduce the Chinese porcelain, white tin glazes were developed with lustre enamel painting over the glaze. This type of ware spread through Byzantium to Europe and across North Africa.

The proximity of Spain and Portugal to North Africa made it inevitable that they should come under the Moorish influence (twelfth century). This influence is particularly evident in the use of lustres and the cladding of buildings with tiles in the Persian tradition. In their turn Spain and Portugal spread the influence still further with the conquest of those parts of South America which were to become colonies in the fifteenth and sixteenth centuries.

In the rest of Europe the ware remained simple but often vigorous. The dusting of lead ore (galena) on to the green ware prior to it being fired was common throughout the Continent in the Middle Ages. Glazed or unglazed engobe designs were the most popular forms of decoration until the introduction of white glazes and later the development of white clays.

The tin glaze which originated in the Near East passed through Spain and then back to Italy via Majorca (hence the alternative name 'majolica'). By the fifteenth century the Italian states were producing a variety of decorated wares with colour painted on to the glaze and fired in the same firing so that the design was protected by the glaze. This technique, together with enamel painting which was painted on to fired glaze, dominated European ceramics until the eighteenth century.

The other significant technical innovation in Europe was that of high-fired stoneware which was glazed with a salt glaze. This was developed in Germany, where there had been a tradition of high-fired ceramics which even when unglazed was superior to the lead-glazed ware common to the rest of Europe.

German Bellarmine bottle in salt-glazed stoneware, c. 1660.

During the sixteenth and particularly the seventeenth century, Chinese porcelain reached Europe as sea trade superseded the overland routes. Tin-glazed pottery began to be painted in Chinese styles and in time the forms tended towards those of the Chinese.

Soon the hunt for a true porcelain was on. The reason for this was both economic and aesthetic. Most of the experiments took place under the status- and revenue-seeking patronage of dukes and princes. The most important centres were Florence, under the Medici in the fifteenth and sixteenth centuries, Meissen under the rulers of Saxony from 1708, Saint-Cloud in France during the seventeenth century, the Royal Danish porcelain factory and Sèvres in France in the eighteenth century.

In England stoneware similar to that made in Germany was produced by John Dwight in London during the eighteenth century and porcelain was being produced at Chelsea by 1750.

While the rest of Europe sought an economic formula for the production of porcelain, in England the search was diverted by the invention of lead-glazed white or cream earthenware. Without royal patronage it was left to individuals like Josiah Wedgwood to develop the art and craft of English ceramics. The famous Wedgwood jasper ware originated about 1770, based on experiments made possible by the fortune he acquired from the manufacture of cream or 'Queen's' ware. As he, and men like him, made fortunes their works expanded to become factories much as we would know them today, producing forms cast in plaster of

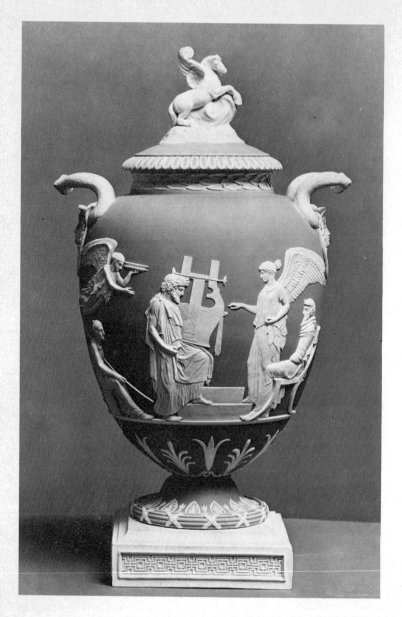

Wedgwood porcelain vase, *The Apotheosis of Homer*, designed by John Flaxman.

(*Opposite, above*) *S. G. White* by Kenneth Price, 1966. Fired and painted clay sculpture.

(*Opposite*) *Aratsa* by Peter Voulkos, 1968. Thrown in two pieces, unglazed.

paris moulds (introduced in 1750) and decorated with printed rather than painted images. Bone china was invented by Spode in 1750 and found a ready market.

With more economic production English wares became cheaper and were exported in great quantities to the rest of the world. While the technical quality of English ceramics remained, the decline in the standards of design of most manufactured objects induced the reaction which has come to be known as the 'crafts revival' in 1860, led by William Morris. This was a search for an improvement in quality through a return to the studio workshop principle of manufacture.

The arts and crafts revival spread through the rest of the industrialized world and re-established contacts with the ceramists in the Far East. It is in this tradition that many Western studio ceramists are working in the present day. In the USA during the 1950s several artists started to work in ceramics in a manner which has come to be known as Abstract Expressionism. Fused by a common experience painters, sculptors and ceramists found new values in each other's forms of expression. Industry has now become divided into either manufacturers of domestic tableware or highly technical developments which are essential to the electrical and engineering industries. The forms and qualities of these industrial objects are having a considerable influence on some ceramists who are making individual pieces today.

2 The nature of clay

In any discussion of the nature of clay it is as well to remember that this material is of natural origin and that it has been formed by geological processes. There is no single analysis for clay.* All clays are mixtures of minerals with a high proportion of 'clay minerals' such as kaolinite.

The Earth as we know it is constantly changing. The landscape we see appears to be fixed and permanent but this illusion belies the fact that over millions of years the world has changed, probably from a hot gaseous mass to a mass with a hot core composed of heavy material enclosed by a crust of solidified material with a light gaseous layer, the atmosphere, surrounding it. The crust is continuous, varies in thickness and is made up of plates rather like an eggshell which has been broken and reassembled. These plates move according to the forces generated beneath them within the molten interior. As they move relatively to each other, earthquakes occur (the San Andreas Fault is one such area) and over a long period mountains may be formed. Where the crust is thin the molten interior may break through from time to time as lava, and form volcanoes. The movement of the crust changes the landscape, which is also weathered by the elements. The transformation is the result of moving material from one place to another, by washing it down streams and rivers and finally into inland lakes or the sea. The beds of these lakes or seas may in time be uplifted once more and so the process may recommence.

A very high proportion of the rocks forming the Earth's crust are of a type known as 'felspathic' (granite is the most commonly known example), that is, they contain in varying proportions the mineral felspar. Where this mineral has been subjected to the action of water the felspar undergoes certain changes, one of which is referred to as 'kaolinization'. In the course of time such rocks decompose to form deposits of kaolin and this is the material from which many clays are formed. Usually these deposits include some impurities as the moving water acts as a carrier for many different minerals. Occasionally steam will emanate from the hot interior of the Earth and where this occurs beneath a felspathic rock the felspar often changes to produce kaolinite. This process, called 'hydrothermal', leaves a very pure type of kaolin deposit (such as the china-clay deposits of Devon and Cornwall in the UK and North Carolina in the USA).

* The following is a selection of definitions:
1 Clay is a fine-grained rock which, when suitably crushed and pulverized, becomes plastic when wet, leather-hard when dried, and on firing is converted to a permanent rock-like mass (American Ceramic Society).
2 Clay: alumino-silicates with many minor but important components.
3 Clay: a natural fusible earth.

Deposits of clay which occur on their site of decomposition are known as 'residual' or 'primary' clays. When such clays are moved by streams, rivers or glaciers to be deposited at another site the resultant deposit is known as a 'sedimentary' or 'secondary' clay.

SEDIMENTARY CLAY DEPOSITS

As water is the commonest agent for the carriage of clay the deposits of sedimentary clay are usually found on the sites of former rivers, lake-beds, estuaries or seas, in fact, anywhere where the velocity of the transporting water may have been decreased. Where the flow of the water is gradually decreased, as may occur where a river enters a lake, the first materials to be deposited are those which are heavy, such as stones and sand; the clay particles, being the lightest of all, are the last to be deposited. On the beds of large lakes clay may be found as relatively pure deposits with the larger particles of clay placed near the mouth of the river and the finer and lighter clay particles further away. Where the river has carried the clay to the sea there may be deposits caused by the flocculating effect of sea water, but inevitably the action of the tides and the waves will have led to the inclusion of sand and similar material into the clay deposits. In those areas of the world which have been subjected to the action of glaciers, clay in common with other material may have been picked up by the ice and moved from its original site. Such a clay is referred to as 'boulder' clay as it contains many stones which are left behind as the glacier withdraws. This clay is usually found mixed with large stones and pebbles.

It should not be assumed from the preceding paragraph that a clay is moved only once in its life. In fact there is evidence that some clays have been transported many times, over thousands of years. Each passage may leave some mark of the transportation either by the impurities or by the

Clay deposit from a river into a lake.

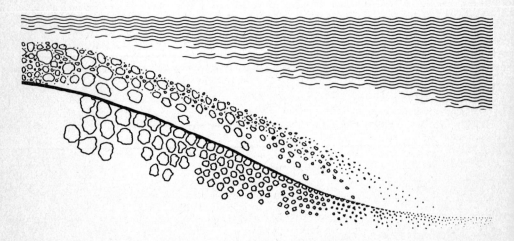

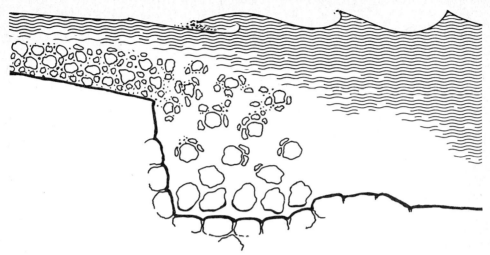

deficiencies in the clay. Pure residual deposits are rare, but sedimentary deposits are many and various. Even in the case of residual clays there are some impurities, so there is no such thing as a deposit of pure clay, but only associations of various clay minerals in association with other minerals. Residual clays are characterized by their refractoriness (they do not melt much below 1,750° C), their relative purity, the white colour of the material when fired and the lack of plasticity. (They do not hold their shape when moulded.)

Sedimentary clays, on the other hand, are plastic but may be anything from white to dark brown in colour when fired, according to the type and quantity of impurities which have been collected during the transportation. They usually melt between 1,150° and 1,500° C. Uncontaminated sedimentary clays known as 'ball' clays are very valuable as additives to residual clays to improve their plasticity without destroying the white-fired colour.

Flocculating and depositing from a river into the sea.

CLAY-MINING

Clays may be mined or dug, according to the exact nature and location of the deposit. Kaolins are usually washed out with high-pressure hoses and drained into settling tanks (or 'blunged') to separate the heavier unwanted material. Sedimentary clays may be dug out of open pits where the clay is firm but not dry, or washed out if it is hard and dry. Beds of clay may appear tilted from their original horizontal deposition and they may vary considerably in depth so that a clay-pit technique may become a deep-mining process as the course of the deposit is followed.

Plasticity is a valuable characteristic and is generated in a clay by the geological action of moving it and reducing the particle size, and then allowing it to settle. The particles of clay may be likened to small plates which, when floated in water and allowed to settle gently, do so slowly, as leaves fall from

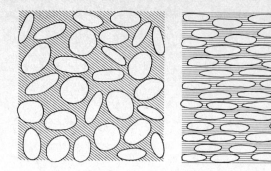

(*Right*) Particle distribution in a residual clay.

(*Far right*) Particle distribution in a sedimentary clay.

trees, always presenting the maximum surface areas to the direction of fall. A residual clay will consist of coarse particles, at many different angles, but a sedimentary clay will have a high proportion of its particles lying in planes parallel to each other as well as being finer-grained. The greater the number of times the clay has passed through this process the fewer will be the particles out of line. This means that the water may pass easily through the mass of clay, coating each particle with a thin film so that when being 'formed' the particles will slide easily over each other and remain in that position during drying and firing.

Conversion of felspar to clay:

KAOLINIZATION	CHEMICAL COMPOSITIONS
felspar	silica, alumina, alkalis
water action	
kaolin	silica, alumina, water, few
decomposition	impurities
residual clay	silica, alumina, water, few
transportation	impurities
sedimentary clay	silica, alumina, water,
	impurities
	smaller particles lying on
	parallel planes

Conversion of felspar to china clay

felspar	silica, alumina, alkalis
hydrothermal action	
kaolinite	silica, alumina, water
decomposition	
china clay	silica, alumina, water

CLAY AND WATER COMBINATIONS

1 There are two main types of water combined with clay: (*a*) water which is chemically combined and is released at temperatures between 225° and 550° C, and (*b*) water which is in free association with the particles of clay. This is released

during the drying process and should be totally removed from the clay at 100° C.

2 A clay mass expands when water is added to it and shrinks when the water is extracted.

3 Fine-grained clays absorb and release water more slowly than coarse-grained clays.

4 Clay masses absorb and release water through the outer surface, so the smaller the mass of clay the more rapid will be the intake and release of free water.

5 There is a point beyond which a clay will not absorb free water without the breakdown of the mass. Beyond this point combinations of clay and water will produce slaked solutions.

6 Hot water will penetrate clays more rapidly than cold water and so accelerate the slaking process.

7 Clays vary in the amount of water they will absorb without slaking.

3 Clay preparation

The last chapter dealt with the methods of removing clays and their associated minerals from the ground. This chapter is concerned with those procedures which should be adopted to ensure satisfactory working properties in the clay. There may be some confusion caused by the various terms which are applied to clays as sold by suppliers. In order to remove this confusion the following terms are given precise definitions.

Clay: any material which includes clay minerals, without regard for its physical properties; usually used to refer to natural clays which are dug from the ground.

Body: natural clays and minerals mixed together to make a material suitable for the making of ceramic forms.

Pastes: bodies which are fired to a point of vitrification, where they are near to collapse. In the case of hard-paste (high-temperature) and soft-paste (low-temperature) porcelains and bone china the fired result is translucent.

It is common these days for ceramists to buy their clays from suppliers, who dig the clay from their own deposits or act as retailers by purchasing many different types of clay, either selling them as dug or mixing them together with different materials to create a body with the desired properties. Any body supplied by a reputable dealer should need very little further preparation to make it suitable for making forms.

The supplier will prepare the raw dug clay by removing any foreign matter. The clay is first broken into convenient nodules and blunged in water. By its rotary mixing action the blunger will render the clay to a solution over a number of hours. In the presence of water the heavier particles will settle to the bottom of the blunger and the lighter clay particles may then be drawn off as a solution of clay and water. This solution is passed through a series of sieves (known as 'screens'). The finest of these sieves may be of 200 mesh and only the finest clay particles will pass through. The fine solution is next passed across an electromagnet which removes any particles of iron that may have been present in the original deposit (or may have come from one of the machines used in a previous process). The clay, still in solution, is passed into a filter press, consisting of a series of cloth bags which hold the clay solution. These bags are squeezed mechanically and the water is drained away. The

clay, which remains in the bags in the form of plastic pan-
cakes, may then be dried and crushed if it is to be sold in
the form of dry clay powder, or it may be passed through
a de-airing pugmill. The pugmill is in three sections: the
first includes a hopper leading to a mixing chamber where
the clay is shredded. The second is a vacuum chamber where
all the air is removed from the clay. This has the effect of
increasing its plasticity, as water flows more easily between
clay particles when air is excluded. The third and final
section tapers towards the exit so that the clay is finally
compressed into a dense homogeneous mass, which comes
from the pugmill in a continuous extrusion. The extrusion
is sliced into convenient lengths and packed into plastic bags
for easy transportation.

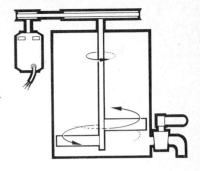

Blunger.

CHANGING THE WORKING PROPERTIES
OF A CLAY

The clay may be improved if, after testing, it is found to be
deficient in one or more of the qualities which would make
it suitable for the manufacture of clay forms.

If it is to be used for throwing, it must be plastic enough to
be formed easily, and hold its shape after forming. It should
not be so plastic that it is slippery and difficult to control,
neither should it shrink excessively or crack during drying.
If a clay is not sufficiently plastic it is said to be 'short'.
Clays which are short can be formed only with difficulty and
tend to crack during the forming process.

Excessively plastic clays, e.g. montmorillonite clays,
should be mixed with short clays to produce a satisfactory
body. The inclusion of minerals with a larger particle size
will often decrease the plasticity and the shrinkage of too
plastic a clay.

Filter press.

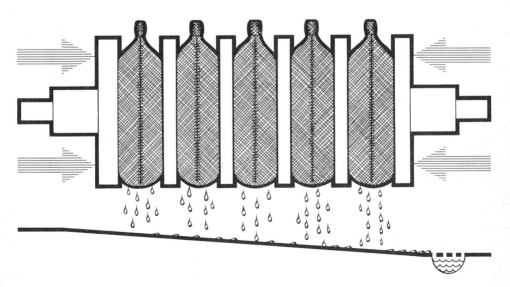

Clays which are too short may be improved by grinding (decreasing the particle size), or weathering, being left exposed to the elements for a long time so that the particles are redistributed by the action of the frost, rain and sun. This is a time-consuming method and is not often used commercially. Other processes include adding a very plastic clay (such as bentonite) or an older clay which has been stored and contains bacterial growth. Lack of plasticity may be due to an excess or shortage of water but this is usually quite apparent. If too much water is present the clay may be dried, but in the case of large masses drying will take place only on the outer surfaces so that the clay must be periodically mixed or 'pugged'.

Pugging through a de-airing pugmill (page 94) will improve the plasticity of the clay, and water may be added during this process. A clay which is to be used in the manufacture of large forms must have a high proportion of coarse material. This may take the form of sand or 'grog' (fired clay which has been crushed and ground to various convenient sizes). This will enable the water, which is necessary for forming of the clay, to evaporate during the drying period.

All clays include some materials which flux during the firing and make the finished ceramic strong and well bonded. If the clay is lacking in sufficient fluxes the fusibility may be increased by the addition of felspar, lead, calcium or mag-

nesium according to the desired maturing temperature, usually in the form of a mineral compound. If the clay is too rich in fluxing agents its refractoriness may be increased by the addition of grog, flint, fireclay or sand. Red-burning clays are the most commonly treated in this way as they all tend to soften too much to be satisfactory at high temperatures.

(Above and opposite) Two nineteenth-century Japanese agate-ware teapots, thrown and modelled in two contrasting clays.

Studio test for workability

It is as well to test any clay which is to be used, even if it has come from a reliable supplier. Each delivery may be quickly tested by rolling some of it into coils, about half an inch in diameter and three inches long, which are bent round to form rings. Several of these should be made, and dried out before firing to the desired temperatures. Glaze reaction to the clay may be tested on these rings or on flat slabs, and any faults which are revealed should be brought to the attention of the supplier.

CHANGING THE COLOUR OF A CLAY

The colour of a clay may normally be changed only by making it darker. For light colours the body clay initially must be white; for dark colours or black a red clay may be used.

29

Dry clay

Slaked clay

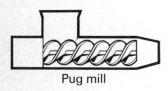
Plaster sink

Pug mill

Clay reclamation.

There are several manufacturers of 'body stains' which can be used to colour clays according to the manufacturer's directions and specifications (see page 180 for list of manufacturers). Traditionally, clays are coloured by the addition of metal oxides, and body stains are compounds of metal oxides and ceramic material.

Suggested oxides and proportions in which they might be added to clay bodies are given below. The larger the percentage of oxide the more intense will be the colour.

OXIDE	%	RESULTANT COLOUR
iron oxide	2 to 6	brown
cobalt oxide	$\frac{1}{2}$ to 3	blue
copper oxide	1 to 4	green
vanadium pentoxide	8 to 11	yellow
iron oxide	3	
cobalt	2	black
manganese oxide	3	

Other oxides may be used to great effect, and experiments with mixtures of several oxides will reveal a wide range of hues and tones. Iron or nickel is usually used to darken a colour and if several oxides are used in a clay it is inadvisable to let them total more than 8 per cent of the weight of the clay, as there is a danger that the metal, acting as a flux, will start to melt the clay when it is fired to a high temperature.

If the coloured clay is to be coated with a glaze, the final colour may be unexpected. Experiments should be undertaken to determine the final colour.

CHANGING THE TEXTURE OF A CLAY

The texture of a clay may be altered for practical or aesthetic reasons. The practical alterations have been dealt with, but additives may be used which change the quality of the clay. There are two types of texture-changing materials: combustible, and refractory.

Combustible materials include sawdust, leaves, ashes or any vegetable matter. They may be wedged (page 81) into the clay or simply pressed into the surface. They will burn away and leave cavities in the fired clay but should not be so large that they cause the clay to crack during drying. It is advisable to keep kilns well ventilated during the firing of such clay.

Refractory materials include sand, pieces of fired clay, grog. These also may be wedged into the clay or pressed upon the surface, and should be of small particle size.

Clay with colouring or texturing additions should be kept separate from other clays to avoid contamination.

It is inevitable that some of the clay which is used to make forms will be wasted, either as part of the process of manufacture or owing to lack of experience and skill. This clay should be stored in plastic bins, a separate bin for each clay so that no contamination can occur. When these bins are two-thirds full, water should be added until the clay is completely covered. After several days the dry clay will have slaked to a muddy consistency and the water which remains on the top can be removed by siphoning. The slurry clay is then scooped out onto shelves, bats or sinks made of plaster of paris or wood. After twenty-four hours the clay will have dried to a plastic state on the underside and should be turned to allow it to dry evenly on all sides. When firm enough to be picked up and still keep its shape, the clay should be pugged or, failing this, wedged by hand until it is again in a state suitable for forming.

Great care should be taken that no foreign matter, especially plaster of paris, is allowed to contaminate working clay (see page 141, 'Plaster spit out').

4 Types of kilns

Kilns are usually identified by the fuel which is burnt to create the necessary heat, but the identification may include the temperature they will attain and the size of the firing chamber. The kiln is the ceramist's major item of equipment. It should be properly fired and maintained to give long and dependable service. In previous times, successful kiln firings depended on skills acquired over many years, but modern kilns are less demanding.

ELECTRIC KILNS

Of all the different types of kiln which may be found in a ceramics studio the most common is the intermittent electric kiln. (The term 'intermittent' indicates that the kiln is heated and then allowed to cool, unlike a tunnel kiln, which is continuously fired and the ware passed through on moving cars.) This usually takes the form of a brick-lined steel box with a door in either the top ('top loading') or the side ('front loading'). The heat is generated by an electric current passing through the wire elements, which are fitted into grooves in the side walls, the floor and sometimes the door. The resistance of the wire causes it to become hot as the current flows. The brick which is used to line the interior of the kiln is called 'insulating brick'; it is very soft and does not withstand harsh treatment, hence the steel casing. The main advantage of this type of brick is that it prevents the heat generated inside the kiln from passing to the outside. There is usually a hole in the roof and one in the door, each fitted with brick plugs (known as 'bungs'). The top bung can be removed during firing to release steam as the clay is heated, and the one in the door may be removed in order to view the interior of the kiln.

This type of kiln can be made in almost any size but if it is considerably higher than it is deep it may be necessary to fit graded elements. Large kilns have more than one hole in the door to view different parts of the kiln and the hole in the top will be bigger and covered by a 'damper', a brick cover which can be opened and closed by a lever on the side of the kiln. These kilns do not require chimneys.

It is relatively simple to manufacture and instal such kilns, and they may be moved to alternative sites without too much difficulty, should this become necessary. As the insulating brick is quite light they are usually prefabricated, and delivered in one piece if access allows. Installation normally consists simply of making electrical connections to a suitable supply.

Kiln atmosphere

The atmosphere in an electric kiln is neutral, that is, there is no consumption of oxygen during the firing, neither is there a flow of air into the kiln to promote an oxygenated atmosphere. Methods of firing this type of kiln are explained below (page 35), but it must be borne in mind that exposed elements are protected by a coating of oxide, which is built up during successive firings. An oxygen-free atmosphere will reduce this coating, leaving a thin and weak element. Unless each reduction firing is followed by at least three neutral or oxidizing firings, there is a likelihood that the elements will fail sooner than expected.

Damage to brickwork

If damage to the brickwork occurs, it is normally on the door or those parts of the sides which have contact with the door, where there is most wear, and the broken pieces can be replaced using a cement supplied by the manufacturer or, if necessary, a commercial fireplace cement. If the wear is

Three electric intermittent kilns. The larger kiln has a single thermocouple, the two smaller kilns one temperature-recording thermocouple and one controlling thermocouple. Beneath each small kiln there is a door switch to cut off the power to the kiln when the door is opened.

Rear view of a test kiln with the back panel removed to reveal two thermocouples, the simmerstat control and ten element terminal blocks. To replace a damaged element, the screws in the terminal block are slackened and the element removed through the front of the kiln.

Element jump: (*top*), the broken element with the piece which is to be inserted; (*bottom*), the element temporarily repaired. Note: this procedure is normally carried out without removing the element from the kiln.

so great that heat is lost during the firing the door may be returned to the manufacturer for a complete rebuild. This should be necessary only after some considerable time.

Element replacement

The failure of one or more elements is usually revealed by the poor performance of the kiln, and on inspection the area of the break will be scarred by charring. Replacing the elements is quite easy. After ensuring that the kiln is isolated from the power supply, the element terminals should be uncovered and disconnected. (The terminals are usually found beneath a metal cover at the back or on the side or door of the kiln, according to the location of the element concerned.) The element may then be removed from inside the kiln. Any charred metal remaining should be cleaned off the brick with a small file. The replacement element should be the one specified by the kiln-manufacturer for that particular location in the kiln. The old element should be measured and the new element (usually supplied in the form of a close-wound spiral) stretched to that same length. The element will have ends made of twisted wire and these should be passed from the firing chamber through the brickwork to the terminals. The connections are then made and the surplus double wire cut off. The rest of the element should be placed in the vacant grooves, ensuring that any bends at the corners are under tension so that they will not become loose, and drop down during firing. The terminal cover may then be replaced and the kiln switched on for a few minutes to check that the element does become warm. If the element does not heat up, either the connections are not secure or another element is in need of replacement.

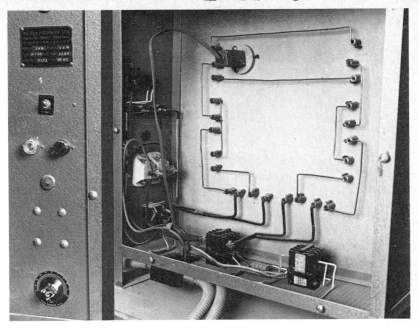

Rear view of a larger kiln, showing two contactors at the base and one thermocouple at the top. The elements are connected in a more complex circuit and the replacement of an element requires the release of the screws in the brass element terminals and withdrawal of the element from the front. On the left of the photograph is an illustration of the side control panel of the kiln. From top to bottom the controls are: soak/off switch, red 'mains on' light, clear 'elements on' light, simmerstat.

In time, all elements will become thin and brittle with successive firings. The thinner the elements become, the longer the kiln will take to reach top temperature. If it is constantly fired to temperatures above those recommended by the manufacturer the life of the elements will be shortened. It is advisable to replace all elements at two-year intervals. If a new element is introduced into a set of older ones an increased strain will be put on the older and thinner elements, causing subsequent failure.

It may sometimes be necessary to 'jump' a break in an element. This can be done quickly but may not last long (sometimes not even the length of a single firing). To do this, a piece of old element is used, broken to the length of the gap plus four coils at either end. The piece is threaded onto one end of the break in the element and pressed into the other so that at least four coils make contact at either end. First attempts to do this may not work but this is usually due to poor contact between the joined pieces.

Elements may be Kanthal wire or Kanthal A1. Kilns fitted with Kanthal wire should not be fired above 1,150° C and those with Kanthal A1 should not exceed 1,300° C. Silicon carbide elements may be fitted where regular and frequent reduction firings are required, but they are expensive.

It is possible to replace one type of element with another but this should be done only by replacing the complete set.

Power regulation

The power into the kiln is regulated by either a simmerstat or a three-way switch. The former proportions the time that the current is permitted to flow and has a dial calibrated from zero to 100. When the dial is set to 50 the current will flow at full rate for 50 per cent of the time. Thus the kiln will be heard to click on and off by the action of a contactor or mercury switch. If the simmerstat is turned to 100 the kiln will remain 'on' all the time. If one or more three-way switches are fitted this will indicate a wiring pattern which allows all the elements to carry current on a 'series' system (low setting), selected elements to carry current on a 'parallel' system (medium setting), or all the elements to carry current in a parallel system (high setting). In a series system, the current passes through one long element which does not get very hot (say 900° C maximum), and in a parallel system the current flows through each element individually, making them much hotter (up to 1,350° C).

The kiln may have some form of heat measuring or controlling equipment but unless a programme controller is fitted the manual simmerstat or three-way switch will be essential.

GAS KILNS

Kilns using gas as a fuel supply are very popular and would, no doubt, be more so were it not for their capital cost. They are cheap to run, require little repair, and provide for a variety of atmospheric conditions within the firing chamber at a wide variety of temperatures. Most gas kilns may be fired to 1,400° C, and do not suffer if reduction firing conditions are induced for all of the firings.

These kilns may be described as brick structures – usually insulating brick within a steel box unless constructed on site, where a steel outer framework only is required – with flues to carry away the burnt gases. The surfaces round the burners are usually of refractory fire-brick to withstand the direct heat of the flames. The hot gases pass around and among the ware and pass through a flue where the rate of exit is controlled by a movable damper.

The gas kilns most commonly designed today are known as 'down-draught' kilns. This simply means that the flames enter the firing chamber at the side, circulate through the stacked forms and exit through flues situated in the base of the firing chamber, from which they are drawn into the chimney, normally situated at the rear of the kiln. Another common design is that known as an 'up-draught' kiln. The flames pass beneath the floor of the firing chamber, up the side and then out of the top of the kiln into the chimney.

A kiln control panel with two three-way switches, a separate floor switch, three 'element on' lamps (one for each switch) and an ammeter to indicate the amount of current flowing through the elements.

A down-draught gas kiln with a trolley hearth. The burning gases rise over the bag walls seen on the right inside the kiln, and exit through the spaces in the floor. The trolley has been pulled out to reveal the two flues at the rear of the kiln through which the spent gases pass into the chimney.

(*Below*) A down-draught kiln: (*left*), sectional front view, showing gas flow; (*right*), sectional side view, showing gas flow.

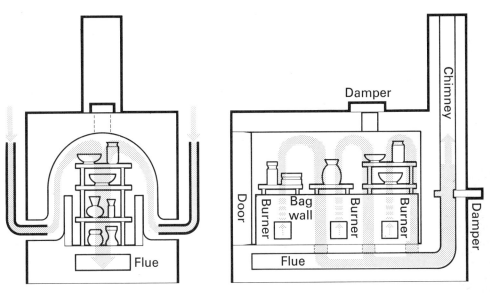

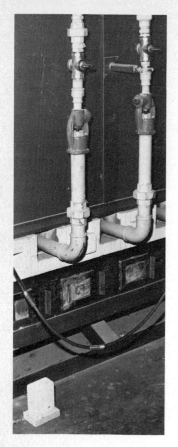

Of these two the most efficient in use of fuel is the down-draught type, but the simplest to build is the up-draught. Small gas kilns may be of the up-draught type but larger kilns (twelve cubic feet upwards) are usually down-draught. If the kiln volume exceeds thirty-six cubic feet it is common to assist the flow and burning of the gases with fan-blown air, which mixes with the gas and in so doing increases its burning efficiency in the firing chamber. The length of chimney for every kiln will be specified by the manufacturer to ensure an adequate draught to pull the spent gases out of the firing chamber. This is more important in the case of natural-draught kilns than with forced-draught types.

Kiln atmosphere

Air, mixed with the gas, enters the kiln through venturi jets and provision is made for more air to flow into the firing chamber by means of secondary air vents situated near the primary gas and air inlet. With the secondary air vents and the damper fully open, complete burning of the gas will take place and the atmosphere is oxidizing, that is to say, the minerals in the bodies and in the glazes will tend to combine to form oxides. When the secondary air vents are shut and the damper partly closed the gases will not burn completely but will seek further oxygen, which will be drawn from the minerals in the ware. The atmosphere in this type of firing is said to be 'reducing', and the minerals in the clay will tend to form oxygen-depleted types.

(*Above*) Burner layout for a gas kiln. From top to bottom, the gas flows down the pipe, past the on/off tap, and through the venturi jet, where it mixes with air and continues down the pipe and into the kiln. The gases are ignited by inserting a gas poker through the hole provided. The secondary air inlet is controlled by a sliding cover beneath the burner pipe.

(*Right*) Up-draught solid-fuel kiln.

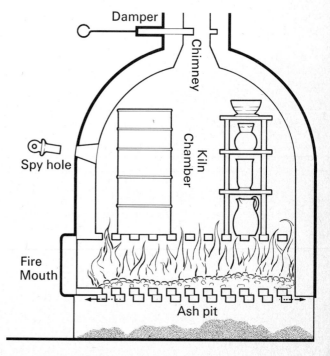

Fuel controls

The flow of gas is regulated by a valve fitted onto the pipe which carries the gas from the mains supply to the kiln. This valve will be graduated by the supplier so that the rate of gas flow at any setting may be clearly seen. Alternatively a water-gauge may be fitted on the pipe leading from the valve to the kiln. This is a glass tube containing water together with a calibrated scale so that as the gas pressure is increased by opening the valve the water column is forced further up the glass tube and the level of the water can be read off against the scale to indicate the precise gas flow. The flow of gas to each burner is regulated by a tap above the venturi jet.

(Above, left) A water gauge for measuring the gas pressure feeding the burners. Behind the gauge are the control valve and the governor which ensures an even pressure of gas from the mains supply.

(Above, right) View of the burners inside the kiln when the bag wall has been partially dismantled. The gases enter through the circular hole in the wall of the kiln and mix with the secondary air entering through the deeper hole. The ignition hole for the gas poker can be seen to the left of the gas inlet.

OIL-FIRED AND SOLID-FUEL KILNS

Oil-burning kilns are of similar design to gas-burning types except that they require different types of burners; these are usually 'drip-feed' or 'air-blown' types.

Coal-, coke- or wood-burning kilns do not have burners, but an open fire either beneath or beside the firing chamber.

The flames are drawn through horizontal flues into the firing chamber. Provision must be made for the removal of ashes produced by the burning of the fuel. This means that either the fuel burns on fire-bars so that the ash falls through and into an ash pit, or the fire must be raked periodically, leaving the burning fuel near the firing chamber and pulling the ash out of the firemouth, thus leaving room for more fuel to be added to the fire.

Large kilns, or those designed for special purposes, may be of the 'moving-hearth' or 'trolley' kiln type. This means that the floor may be pulled out on rails or free-running wheels for easier loading. 'Top-hat' kilns are those in which the hearth is fixed but the top and sides may be raised mechanically so that there is easy access around the loading area. This type is rare in small workshops.

Continuous or tunnel kilns are usually found only in factories. The ware is moved through the kilns on fire-proof trollies and the kiln becomes progressively hotter towards the middle and cooler towards the end. These kilns are usually maintained at running temperature for months, hence the name 'continuous kilns'.

The above kilns may be fired by any fuel, but 'top-hat' kilns are usually electric and tunnel kilns are usually gas- or oil-fired.

SITE SURVEYS

Before ordering a gas kiln the site should be surveyed (by a Gas Board official in the UK or a representative of the company supplying the gas in the USA) to ensure that the mains supply is capable of providing the gas flow which the manufacturer specifies as necessary for the kiln in question. There should be no danger of gas leaks and consequent explosion, provided that the kiln is installed by a competent fitter and the mains supply is turned off when the kiln is not in operation.

Oil-burning kilns will require storage tanks adjacent to the kiln site, large enough to contain at least enough fuel for a complete firing (and some to spare in an emergency). Some storage space will also be required for the fuel for solid-fuel-burning kilns.

All kilns which burn fuel require chimneys to draw the gases into the atmosphere. Siting of such chimneys may be subject to planning approval by the local authorities. Electric kilns do not require chimneys but the top vent should be at least eighteen inches away from the ceiling of the room. Kilns are often heavy and the floor of the kiln site must be strong enough to withstand the weight.

5 Temperature and heat work measurement

One of the difficulties that the ceramist encounters is that he can never tell exactly how the forms, in the kiln, are being changed until they have cooled. Before the invention of the devices that are used today, ceramists set test pieces in the kiln in such positions that they could be removed at various stages of the firing ('draw trials'). In this way experience was acquired of the characteristics of each kiln, and the rate of stoking needed to achieve the desired qualities in the ware. In time, the man responsible for the firing of each kiln became sufficiently skilled to tell the state of the firing, from the colour inside the kiln as seen through the spyhole, and the length and colour of the flames emanating from the flue. Draw trials are still used, especially when reduction effects are being sought, as there is still no device for determining the amount of oxygen present in the kiln atmosphere. The disadvantages of draw trials alone are that they do not give any indication of the rate of increase in temperature in the kiln, and they may be dislodged and fall onto the other forms being fired.

PYROMETRIC CONES

Pyrometric cones are used to measure the heat input into kilns. They soften and bend at temperatures determined by their formulation, which can be identified by numbers impressed on the side of the cone (see page 176 for a list of cone numbers and their squatting temperatures). By placing three of these cones in the kiln, in such a position that they may be seen through a spyhole, and selected to bend at 30° C intervals, sufficient warning may be given of the approach of the finishing temperature. These cones are widely used as they measure the 'heat work' to which the clay has been subjected, rather than the temperature of the firing. It is possible to overfire a kiln by firing too slowly to a predetermined temperature, thus allowing too much reaction to take place between the ingredients in the clay and the glaze. Conversely, it is possible to underfire the kiln by firing to the same temperature too quickly, thereby not allowing sufficient time for the reactions. Pyrometric cones accurately measure this time/temperature ratio, which is referred to as 'heat work'.

PYROMETERS

Pyrometers are commonly used to measure the temperature within the kiln. They consist of two parts, a galvanometer (a device for measuring very small electric currents) and a thermocouple (a pair of dissimilar metals joined at the end and protected by a porcelain sheath). The thermocouple is connected to the galvanometer within the pyrometer by a length of compensating cable.

The thermocouple is placed in the wall or top of the kiln so that the end projects three to four inches into the firing chamber. When heat is applied to the tip of the thermocouple a small electric charge is generated in each metal. A further charge is generated between the hot and cold ends of one of the wires. Measuring both types of induced charge, it will be found that the current will vary uniformly as the temperature rises, and this may be read on a calibrated

Pyrometric cones (*top*) and a pyrometer and thermocouple. At the bottom of the illustration are the elements which make up a thermocouple, the outer porcelain sheath which supports the twin metal strips inside the kiln, the connection block and the metal casing.

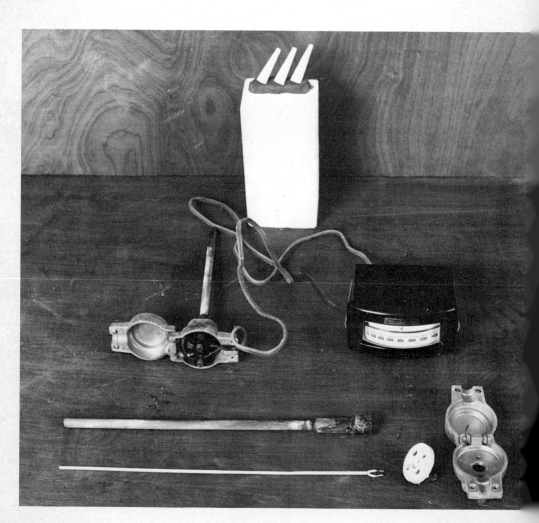

scale on the pyrometer. To produce accurate results the following rules must be observed:

1 Do not change the length of compensating cable as the pyrometer is calibrated to compensate for any electrical resistance in this cable.

2 Set the pyrometer at room temperature (using the zero adjuster provided on the instrument), not at zero.

3 Do not allow the cold end of the thermocouple accidentally to become warm during use.

4 The porcelain sheath and the metal wires inside it are fragile and expensive. Use great care when removing or installing this unit.

5 The pyrometer is delicate and should not be removed from the system without a shunt wire (fuse wire will do) to connect the two terminals.

6 The system depends on electric current, so ensure that connections to the various terminals are the right way round, i.e. negative to negative, positive to positive.

7 Do not confuse the thermocouple with a heat fuse (if fitted), and never pass mains current through the thermocouple.

A visual controlling pyrometer. The knob on the left determines the position of the control needle (the lower one beneath the scale). The light on the left of the scale indicates the flow of mains current to the controller and that on the right the flow to the elements.

If the system fails or becomes inaccurate, either the pyrometer must be returned to the manufacturer or the thermocouple wires must be replaced, if they have been broken. These are usually salvageable and, if returned to the supplier, their value may be credited against the cost of replacement. Sheaths are less expensive and break easily if exposed to careless handling.

Generally this system of pyrometer and thermocouple is expensive to buy, but should last many years if used with care. There is no better way of accurately measuring the temperature rise and fall throughout a kiln firing.

CONTROLLERS FOR ELECTRIC KILNS

There are several types of these, varying in cost according to the degree of sophistication of the instrument. They are based upon the system of a thermocouple within the kiln and a pyrometer. The mains power supply is passed through a switch device (controlling the fuel input) which is switched via contactors by the pyrometer.

Controlling pyrometer

This instrument gives a reading of the kiln temperature but has the facility of a second needle on the dial which can be moved by the operator to the desired temperature. When the temperature-reading needle coincides with the final temperature needle, the kiln will either switch off or remain soaking (i.e. held at that temperature) according to the position of the soak–off switch.

ETHER 'Mini'   Type 19·90

A non-indicating controller. The scale is rotated to bring the red pointer in line with the desired temperature. The light at the top indicates mains flow to the controller; that on the right remains on until the kiln has reached the desired temperature and comes on again when the temperature falls below.

(*Opposite*) A recorder (*top*) which draws a chart of the progress of the kiln firing, and a programme controller (*bottom*). The lamps at each side of the scale indicate 'mains on' (*left*) and current flow to the elements (*right*). The pointer below the scale is moved by the rotating cam seen through the panel below. The switch in the top left-hand corner of the bottom panel switches on or off the motor for the cam. In the off position, the kiln will hold the set temperature indefinitely. Behind the cam a movable arm may be positioned so that it will move round with the cam and will switch off the kiln as it passes the marker in the bottom left-hand corner.

Non-indicating controllers

These are simpler and cheaper than controlling pyrometers but do not give instant and accurate readings of the kiln temperatures throughout the firing; they cut off the power supply or soak the kiln at the desired temperature.

In both the above controlling systems the rate of rise of the temperature of the kiln must be controlled by a simmerstat or similar device.

Programme controllers

Only a programme controller will control the rate of rise, the final temperature and the length of soak. This instrument consists of a thermocouple within the kiln, connected to a controlling pyrometer, which has a control needle that is moved across the face of the pyrometer at a rate determined by a motor-driven cam. If the pyrometer indicates that the kiln temperature exceeds that shown by the control needle the kiln will switch off until the control needle moves to indicate a higher temperature. The shape of the cam determines the rate of rise, the highest temperature reached and the length of soak (if any).

Time clocks

Time clocks are useful as they can start the kiln firing without an operator being present (all the above types require to be manually started). If the exact time for the kiln to reach temperature is known, a time clock can be used to switch off the kiln.

Heat fuses

Heat fuses may be used in electric kilns. But these are convenient only for protecting the kiln from damage if overfired. A heat fuse looks like a thermocouple but is wired to the mains supply. If the kiln overfires, the wire in the heat fuse melts, thus cutting off the power to the kiln before the elements melt.

Kiln sitters

Where the kilns are situated in educational establishments it is well worth the expense (which can be quite modest) of fitting a simple cut-out device such as a kiln sitter. This is a device where the power input is passed through a switch. The switch is held in the 'on' position by a pyrometric cone, chosen to correspond with the temperature required, projecting into the firing chamber. When the pyrometric cone softens, the switch can spring to the closed position, cutting off the power supply to the kiln.

44

A bank of kilns and controllers. The controller on the left controls the larger kiln and the single controller to the right works the two small test kilns. The switch boxes in the background enable the controller to operate both small kilns in turn.

CONTROLLERS FOR GAS- AND OIL-FIRED KILNS

In the case of gas- and oil-fired kilns, controllers are very expensive as solenoid valves must be fitted to control or cut off the fuel flow as required, instead of electrical contactors. Each system is designed for each kiln in its environment. It is too complex and expensive to make the fitting of controllers to solid-fuel kilns worthwhile.

The colour of the interior of the kiln can be used as an approximate guide to the temperature (see page 177).

Controllers are much used in industry to achieve constant repetition of firing conditions. In educational establishments they release staff for the more valuable role of teaching and allow for overnight and week-end firing without supervision, thus increasing the number of firings possible in a week. They also serve as guardians over 'forgotten' kilns when a crisis occurs elsewhere. For the studio ceramist they increase the usage of expensive capital and equipment, and tend to increase element life, in the case of electric kilns, by standardizing the firing programme.

There is today a wide variety of controllers at prices which should allow for the more extensive use of this invaluable equipment.

In most studios, kilns are set with more than one heat-measuring system, e.g. pyrometer and thermocouple to read the temperature rise and pyrometric cones to measure heat work. Should either system fail, then the kiln need not be fired 'by guess and by God' and time and energy spent on the ware is not in danger of being lost.

6 Hand tools for forming clay

A wide variety of tools are used in the making, finishing and modelling of ceramic forms. This chapter will permit only a brief survey of those in common use. These can often be made without much difficulty but those that require special skills or equipment should be purchased from commercial suppliers. These days it is possible to buy all necessary tools, but apart from their cost they tend to be compromises of the most popular shapes and materials. Students of ceramics may soon find that the only way to achieve the form of tools they need will be to make them.

Forming tools fall into three categories: (1) those which may be considered as extensions and refinements of the fingers; (2) those which cut the clay in some way; (3) those which produce textures and shapes by being pressed against the clay.

MODELLING TOOLS

These may be made of wood, metal or plastic. *Wooden tools* should be made from hard, fine-grained wood which will not splinter or break during use. The shapes to be made will depend on the use to which they are to be put. The simplest to make and the cheapest to buy are those made from flat pieces of wood, with two opposite sides cut to the required shape and the sharp edges sanded smooth. Those tools which are modelled in the round take longer to make and are more expensive to buy. Bamboo sharpened to a point, or wedge-shaped, is useful for incising lines in plastic clay. Large wooden beaters resemble modelling tools in design but are used to beat the clay and compress it to the desired form. They are commonly used to refine the form of hand-built clay shapes and may be clad in fabric to produce textured surfaces which help to prevent the beater from sticking to the clay.

Plastic tools may be made in much the same way as wooden tools except that they can also be shaped by heating the plastic and bending it by hand or over a preformed surface. Thermoplastics, such as perspex, are a most suitable type of plastic as they are malleable in the heated state and firm when cooled. Plastic tools are strong, can be completely smooth and are easily shaped.

Metal tools are not easily formed and are expensive to buy, but they are ideal for modelling hard clay and plaster. Stainless-steel tools are very expensive but will not stain the clay or plaster with small deposits of iron. Neither will they corrode – an important factor as clay is a very corrosive material.

Modelling tools usually are differently shaped at each end. These may be spatulated for smoothing, serrated for texturing, blunt and narrow to model small grooves, or knife-edged to incise the clay.

CUTTING TOOLS

Wires are the most common cutting device used in a ceramics studio. The wire may be of copper, bronze, stainless steel or nylon, but metal wires cut more precisely than nylon. Twisted wires may be used as well as single strands. No wire will last for ever and a stock of replacement wires should be maintained.

Harps are cutting wires which are fastened across the open end of a U-shaped metal frame. The legs of the U should be notched at intervals to prevent the wire from slipping off the open end. These notches will allow the wire to be placed at various distances from the end of the frame. With this cutting tool it is possible to cut horizontally through a pancake of clay. If the harp is held vertically so that the legs are pressed onto the surface on which the clay is lying throughout the cutting movement, the wire will cut the clay to an even thickness. Interesting surfaces may be cut into blocks of clay using a harp and moving it up and down, across and round.

Cutting wires which are not set into frames should be fitted with toggles which should be tied securely to the ends of the wire. With these it should be possible to exert considerable force on the wire without harming fingers or hands. Cutting wires of this type are used to slice through blocks of clay, and slabs too wide to be cut with a harp.

Flutes are wood or metal tubes, cut in half longitudinally, with a slot cut across the rounded surface, very like the air slot in a flute or whistle. This produces a curved-section groove, when drawn across a clay surface. The cutting action is similar to that of a wood gouge.

Knives are frequently used. The blade should be flexible and firmly attached to the handle. They may be narrow with a gradually tapering blade for fine work such as fettling, or broad and flat like painters' palette-knives for grinding colours. Ordinary kitchen knives are suitable if their blades can be safely ground to the required shape.

Hole-cutters are made from metal tubes. A length of tube about five inches long with the end cut at an acute angle will provide a pointed cutting tool. Tubes of various sizes will be useful in providing a selection of varied hole-cutters.

A selection of modelling and turning tools: (*left, top to bottom*), steel modelling tools, a needle, two wire-ended turning tools, three turning tools (leaf, triangular, and round-ended), wooden and plastic modelling tools; (*right*), two rubber kidneys, two steel scrapers, two grades of hacksaw blades and two knives.

Needles are useful to cut clay, especially during the throwing process. They should be secured to wooden handles, to make them not only easier to hold but also easier to find when covered in clay.

Pastry-cutters bought from a hardware shop can be used to stamp out shapes from either flat slabs or hollow forms. Metal ones are sharper and give a better finished edge. These cutters can be found in a variety of sizes.

More sophisticated cutters of this type may be bought from ceramic suppliers. They are usually of the type which has a spring-loaded back plate so that the clay can be pushed out of the cutting frame without distorting it.

Turning tools may be regarded as cutting tools but their action is better described as 'paring'. They may be wire-ended or of flat steel. Wire-ended tools are probably better bought, but can be made. Steel tools are made out of flat strips of steel about quarter of an inch thick. The ends should be turned at right angles and then ground to the required shape and given a bevelled cutting edge.

Some larger wire-ended tools may be used to produce clay coils by drawing them through blocks of clay.

Bamboo cut to a length of eight inches, with its thickness reduced by half at one end, may be bent round on itself to form a turning tool with a looped end. The bamboo will give a very sharp cutting edge.

SHAPING AND TEXTURING TOOLS

Profiles are either used to form the clay into an exact shape in the throwing and turning process, or pulled across slabs of clay to produce textures, shapes and patterns. The usual materials for profiles are wood and metal. They are usually made by the ceramist, but simple curved bamboo throwing profiles can be purchased.

It is important that the profile be designed to provide an ample grip when held in the hand, or tool-holder if used. The cutting edge should be bevelled on the leading edge to avoid tearing the clay.

Moulds may be made of plaster or clay which has been formed and then bisquited (see page 115). Clay pressed into such a mould and then applied to a clay form is called a 'sprig'.

Stamps are used to impress directly on the surface of the clay form. Potters' stamps with trade-marks or initials may be made of plaster of paris, wood, metal or bisquited clay.

The following are not really forming tools but small ancillary items. *Sponges* are of two types – natural and synthetic. Natural sponges are expensive but there is no satisfactory substitute for throwing or press moulding clay and soaping plaster. Synthetic sponges are cheaper and may be used to clean glaze from bisquited clay, work surfaces and other abrasive surfaces which would tear a natural sponge.

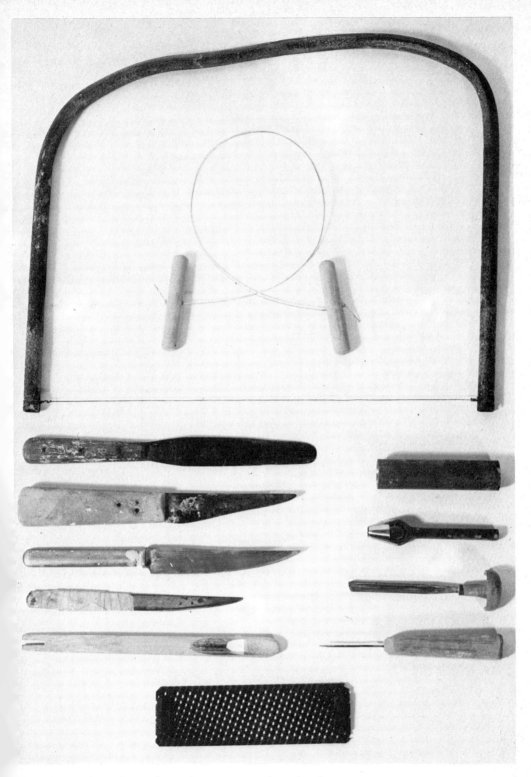

Clay cutters: *top to bottom*, a harp and a cutting wire with toggle ends; *left*, a palette knife, two general-purpose knives, a fettling knife made from a hacksaw blade, and a flute; *right*, three hole-cutters and a needle; *bottom centre*, a pierced file blade.

Coarse files and planes of various types are ideal for scraping leather-hard or dry clay. The clay has a tendency to block the cutting surface so the type of file which has perforations through the cutting surface is the most useful as it tends to be self-cleaning. Files can be used to clean any rough edges from soft-fired clay.

Rolling-pins come in various sizes. There is no need to buy proper rolling-pins, sold for baking, for any large-diameter round wood will do. Discarded dinghy masts and oars are two examples of the kind of object which can be cut to suitable lengths to serve as rolling-pins. Metal tubes are not usually heavy enough and the clay tends to stick to the surface, so they are not ideal for rolling out the clay. Textures and patterns may be pressed into the clay with the aid of textured rolling-pins. Plaster of paris can be cast in cardboard tubes so that when the cardboard is removed the plaster provides a surface which may be cut or carved to produce a textured roller.

Guides are used to determine the depth of clay slabs. They should be available in pairs of identical thickness and are usually made of wood. It is useful to drill countersunk holes in each guide so that it may be secured to the laying-up surface on the modelling-board with the aid of screws. In this way, when clay is placed between the guides, the rolling-pin or cutting wire will move smoothly across them, producing slabs of uniform thickness.

Boards are used for all sorts of purposes, from laying up clay to carrying forms to and from the kiln. They should be light enough to be carried by one person when fully laden. Laying-up boards may be cast in plaster of paris, otherwise boards are normally made of timber or blockboard.

Release agents. Damp clay will stick to most surfaces unless prevented from doing so. Flint or fine sand may be used on flat surfaces or damp flint alone on rough vertical surfaces. Special precautions must be taken in the use of these materials, as the inhalation of flint or fine sand can cause silicosis or other respiratory diseases. Avoid methods of spreading these materials (such as vigorous sieving) which might lead to their being dispersed as a fine dust in the atmosphere of the studio. If damp clay is found to stick to a metal surface, rape-seed oil applied to the metal can sometimes assist in releasing the clay. Any release agent will have to be reapplied each time fresh clay is placed on the surface.

Hessian or some similar fabric will not only serve to prevent the clay from sticking to the surface but may also prove useful when the clay has to be lifted from the laying-up board onto a moulding surface (see page 63), and should enable the clay to be moved without cracking. If it is used in conjunction with wooden guides, the fabric should be placed between the guides and the board with the fixing screws passing through the fabric to prevent it moving as the clay is cut or rolled flat.

7 Hand methods of forming clay

Clay forms which are made by hand are characterized by irregularities in the form, surface and section. Typical examples of such work include pottery containers, tiles, bricks and sculptures. In a society where the skills of hand forming have been developed the resultant work may be mistaken for mechanically constructed forms. In particular the large storage containers from the Middle East display considerable regularity, as do contemporary African wares. In many ways they represent an economy of means and material, together with a richness of form which can still arouse the admiration of ceramist and layman alike. These methods are ideal for the novice as there is a direct confrontation between maker and material with the opportunity to achieve sophisticated results.

Clays for hand forming should include some coarse material such as sand or grog, but should otherwise be of average plasticity. The particle size should be large enough to allow the water to pass easily through the clay during drying, as the section will probably be uneven, with the possibility that an apparently dry surface will conceal pockets of water where the clay is thicker.

When joining two pieces of clay it is essential that they be of similar thermal expansion and dampness so that they shrink at similar rates, thus avoiding their cracking apart. It is as well to eradicate all signs of joining so that a smooth surface results wherever possible. This lessens the ever-present danger of joins opening, and the form coming apart, during firing.

The clay may be of any colour, either natural or pigmented (see page 29). Stoneware and earthenware clays are commonly used but porcelain and bone china are not usually regarded as hand-building clays because it is extremely difficult to achieve the thinness and regularity of section necessary for the body to appear translucent in the fired state, and the particle size is too small to allow proper drying to occur safely. Nevertheless it is possible to use these clays if the object is very small, and great care is taken.

The clay in a damp plastic state may be pinched, rolled, squeezed or modelled by hand, with tools or by using its quality to accept impressions of other objects. Such modelling may be on slabs of any shape, in relief, flat or in the round according to the inclination of the maker. Chapter

10 deals with methods of changing clay surfaces. It will be noted during the operation that damp, leather-hard and dry clays have different modelling characteristics.

PINCHING

Small pots may be formed by rolling the clay into a ball, and while holding this in the left hand, placing the thumb of the right hand in the centre and applying pressure by thumb and fingers as the left hand rotates the clay. The clay will be squeezed into the form of a crude pot. If this procedure is repeated rhythmically, and less and less pressure applied as the clay becomes thinner, quite delicate forms may be made. Pots made by this method are called 'thumb pots' or 'pinched pots'.

COILING

Materials and tools: wooden board, hessian or flint, rolling-pin, knife, clay, modelling tools.

Methods: First, decide the size of the form to be made as this will determine the thickness of the base and the walls. As a rough guide, if the pot is to be eighteen inches high the base should be at least half an inch and at most one inch thick. The walls should be the same thickness as the base, but may be thinner at the top as they need to support less weight.

(*Below*) A coil pot complete, and another just being started:

Coiling being used as the basis of a form, which is smoothed with a template.

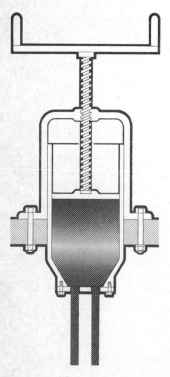

A wad-box extruding coils through a die.

Roll out a piece of clay of suitable size for the base of the form to the correct thickness on a board with a piece of hessian or some flint between the clay and the board. The rest of the clay is rolled by hand or extruded through a wad-box or pugmill with suitable die plates, to provide a series of coils out of which the walls may be made. The coils should be about one and a half times thicker than the finished walls are to be, and preferably long enough to go round the form so that there is only one join in each layer. Making even coils by hand is more difficult than may appear. If each coil is rolled on a wooden surface or one that is covered with fabric, and rolled at least one revolution, using the palms of the hands, then with a little practice the technique should be fairly easily mastered. If more than one or two coils are prepared they should be covered with a damp cloth until just before they are required.

Join the first coil by placing it round the top of the base and cutting off any excess length so that it fits exactly. Lay the next coil on to the first in the same manner and so on until four or five coils are in place. It is important that the joins in each coil do not lie one above the other as this would make for a weakness in the structure. If each coil is placed so that the join occurs on successive quarters of the clock the joins will occur one above the other only every fourth layer. To join the coils to each other, and to the base, 'pull down' a small piece of each coil on to that underneath, repeating this with each coil right round the outside of the form and then on the inside. This can by itself produce an interesting surface but if a smooth finish is desired the form may be beaten when leather-hard or scraped when dry. If the coils are themselves to be the finished surface, the 'pulling down' may be done on the inside only. Continue

Early twentieth-century East African gourd-shaped vessel, coiled, modelled and burnished with graphite.

the process of building up the coils until the form is completed. If a widening form is required, the coils should be made progressively longer and each one, when placed on its predecessor, should be placed so that it overhangs slightly.

A form of any size can be constructed by the coiling method, but the diameter of the coils should be increased in the case of forms more than twelve inches high.

If the coiled form is to be beaten, this should only be done when the form is leather-hard. Wooden beaters which have a textured or patterned surface will often produce rich and exciting surfaces.

In some cases the form may be of such a shape or size that it is necessary to construct it in stages, either by making it in several pieces and joining them together at the leather-hard stage or by constructing the lower portion of the form and leaving it to dry to leather-hard, while keeping the topmost coil plastic with a damp cloth. It may be necessary to support the form by filling it with crumpled newspaper or by propping up the outer surface with a clay collar. If newspaper is used, it can be left inside the form as it will burn away during the firing. When the lower portion of the form is dry and strong enough to support the subsequent layers, remove the damp cloth and continue the coiling process until the form is complete or shows signs of collapse – in which case it should be allowed to dry again, but always ensuring that the top coil is kept damp so that it will bond to the subsequent layers.

Mexican teapot vessel. Modelled and painted, unglazed.

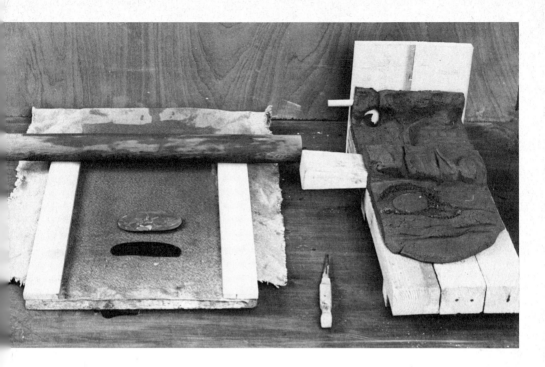

The coiled form may be scraped or planed in a leather-hard or dry state to produce a more controlled surface and shape.

The layout for a slabbing, together with a slab in a later stage of being formed and modelled.

SLABBING

This is a technique which is suitable for making angular, flat-faced forms such as boxes. The method is quite simple and is suitable for any size of faceted object.

Clays for slabbing should be fairly coarse-grained if the form is to be greater than six inches in any dimension. Large forms which exceed eighteen inches in one dimension should be made of coarse clay such as fireclay.

Tools: modelling-board or plaster slab, rolling-pin and guides or harp, ruler, knife, paper patterns, hessian or flint.

Method: firstly, the board should be covered with fabric or a dusting of flint to prevent the clay sticking to the wood. There should be enough room on the board or boards for all the faces of the form to be laid out at the same time, thus ensuring that they will maintain a common water content at every stage of the construction. Fix the wooden guides to the boards with screws so that they may be removed without difficulty. The size of the form to be made must be decided upon and the suitable clay placed upon the board.

A plaster slab may be substituted for the wooden board. This has the advantage that the clay will not stick to the plaster and will shrink evenly on both surfaces, but guides to

Plaster laying-up or slip-casting slab.

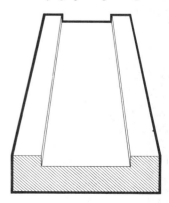

Slabs being used to produce a box form.

determine the thickness of clay cannot be fixed satisfactorily to plaster, though it is possible to cast them into the plaster block. Roll the clay flat on the board using the guides or a harp as necessary, and then smooth the clay surfaces with a rubber 'kidney' or a flexible steel scraper. The shapes to be cut should be measured on the clay, or you can use paper patterns to measure and shape the pieces accurately. Cut out the clay shapes on the boards and remove and discard the spare clay. The pieces to be used are put to dry until they are leather-hard and stiff enough to be handled without being deformed. At this stage they must be turned over so that each face dries evenly. If this is not done the top-side may dry and shrink more than the under-side, resulting in a warped slab.

When they are leather-hard, prepare the pieces by cutting them to the exact size. The edges should be trimmed at this stage, if mitred joints are desired. Score the edges in a cross-hatch pattern, and spread slurry over the cross-hatching. Normally the pieces are assembled by fixing one of the sides to the base and then joining the other pieces in the most convenient order. The pieces to be joined are cross-hatched and slurried, placed together and gently moved up and down against each other until they lock. Increasing resistance will be felt as the pieces are moved against each other and this is a sign that the join is good. Any slurry squeezed out in this process should be cleaned off.

As an alternative to using slurry, where finer results are required, it is sometimes preferable to use only water. This is quite safe provided the clay is cross-hatched in the usual way and water applied to the surfaces to be joined. The first two pieces are placed together and moved gently up and down against each other. Some of the clay particles will

break away from the slabs and form a slurry with the water within the join. As with the slurry method, an increasing resistance will be felt as the joint bonds.

With large objects it is advisable to reinforce each join with a coil of clay on the inside. This has the effect of rounding off the interior corners so that the stresses which build up

Chinese model of a house, Han Dynasty. Slab-built, modelled and painted, unglazed.

during drying and firing pass through the wall of clay and do not focus on the corners, which are the weakest points in a slab-built form.

It is possible to use slabs in a freer manner by constructing while they are still soft. This is an exciting method to use but there is a risk of their cracking apart at a later stage. The amount of control which can be exercised is somewhat limited until there has been a great deal of practice. But all this may add to the spontaneity inherent in objects made in this way. It may not be necessary to use a cross-hatch and slurry join if the pieces of clay are soft enough to form a bond when pressed well together.

PRESSING

This is a method very similar in some cases to that of slip-casting (see page 76) except that the clay in this case is plastic, and stronger in the dry state. It was a method widely used in industry for large shapes and forms where slip-casting would be too demanding of labour or technology.

Tools: modelling-board covered with hessian or flint, rolling-pin and guides or a harp, knife, mould or moulding surface, sponge.

Method: roll the clay or cut it into thin slabs and smooth it in the same manner as with slabbing (see page 59). If there is any possibility of the clay sticking to the moulding surface, treat it with a resist such as flint. If the form is complex, with the possibility that the clay may lock in position in the mould when pressed in one piece, it may be necessary to press the clay in small pieces, remove them from the mould when leather-hard and join them together, as with slabbing.

Pressing clay into a simple mould.

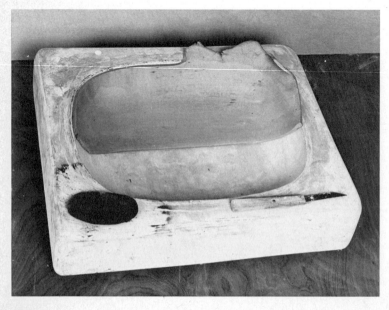

Self-portrait by Peter Palmer. Press-moulded fireclay, cut from an eight-piece mould and reconstructed on the kiln trolley hearth.

When the clay has been rolled out it should be lifted into the mould. This may necessitate the mould being placed on to the clay and then turning the laying-out board, hessian, clay and mould upside-down, before removing the board and hessian. With a damp sponge ease the clay into position, taking great care not to stretch it too much, as it may tear or become too thin to withstand firing. When the clay has been eased into position it can be pressed firmly into the mould to produce a satisfactory reproduction of the mould surface. Trim off any excess with a knife, and when the clay is leather-hard, remove it from the mould. Any unwanted marks or folds in the clay may then be filled or smoothed out.

The choice of mould is a personal one, but there are several different types. The mould may require that the clay be pressed over it or it may be hollow and the clay pressed into it. It may be a round object selected for its form or surface, or it may be made for the purpose in either wood, clay (which has been formed and fired to bisquit) or plaster. Any number of pieces may be moulded and joined together to make more complex forms.

(*Opposite*, *above*) Various handles: a plaited handle (*left*) and three pulled handles.

(*Opposite*, *below*) Three shards showing various handles with thumb stops.

(*Top*) Pressing clay over a mould.

(*Above*) The clay form trimmed and finished.

Hump moulds are favoured by ceramists in the production of engobe-coated forms. The surface coated with engobe is in contact with the moulding surface during this process and should be almost leather-hard before it is formed on the mould.

PULLING

This method, used almost exclusively for making handles for thrown forms, is really a combination of pulling and smoothing. No tools are needed if the process is carried out near a sink, otherwise a large bowl of clean water is required.

The procedure is as follows. Choose clay which is the same as that from which the thrown form is made, wedge it

carefully, shape it into a carrot form, and place it on the edge of a convenient shelf so that two-thirds of the clay overhangs. With wet hands, pull this by moving the thumb and forefinger down the clay, from the thick end to the thin, so that the form becomes elongated.

Gradually a thin strip of clay will be produced; the section of this will be concave if the thumbs are placed to pull down the centre, or the section may include a spine if the two thumbs are placed to the edges of the strip and pulled down simultaneously. When it is pulled to slightly more than the desired length, pinch off the clay handle at the thicker end and place it on a board to stiffen. Great care should be taken when the clay is in this very soft state as it is susceptible to accidental damage. When slightly softer than leather-hard, the handle may be curved into shape and then fitted to the clay form.

Unglazed red earthenware jar, thrown, with three pulled handles. Glazed on the inside.

8 Slip casting

Slip casting, like press moulding, utilizes moulds to reproduce forms. The slip is a solution of clay and water which, when poured into a porous mould, will deposit a layer of plastic clay against the sides of the mould. The fact that the slip is liquid allows for the reproduction of more complex shapes than is possible with plastic clay. The process is attended by several problems which can be difficult to resolve but nevertheless is much favoured as an industrial technique because it lends itself to the division of labour. There are several quite different skills involved in the design and manufacture of satisfactory moulds, the formulation and blending of the slip and the handling and finishing of the cast pieces. In a studio, however, it is generally considered too time-consuming to produce moulds unless at least a dozen identical pieces are to be reproduced. In some cases, however, slip casting will be the only possible method of reproducing the desired form, as is often the case when found and man-made objects formed in another material are to be reproduced in all their detail.

The form round which the mould is to be made, called a 'model', may be made of any material. If the mould is carefully and properly made it should produce cast forms which are identical to the model in every way. The mould is normally made from plaster of paris but sand may be used in certain circumstances (see page 72). Sand moulds are usually destroyed when the cast is removed. This, together with the texture of the cast pieces, makes sand unsuitable for the production of many forms.

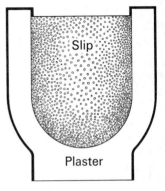

Slip casting in a porous mould.

PLASTER OF PARIS

The use of plaster of paris for moulds became common in the eighteenth century. It is made by heating gypsum to 107° C so that some of the chemically combined water is driven off. When water is added to the resulting powder a creamy liquid is produced which cures naturally to form a hard, porous mass. The plaster must be fresh; if it is stored for a long time it will absorb airborne water and will not cure to a hard mass when more water is added. Heat is a by-product of the curing process. As the plaster cures it also swells, and this has the effect of pressing the still soft plaster hard against the model and picking up even the slightest detail. The curing stage is complete when the plaster has cooled. When cool it returns to its original volume, thus facilitating removal from the model.

Liquid plaster must be contained in the desired shape until it has 'gone off', that is, when it has cooled, after becoming hot during the curing process. The containing walls, called 'cottles', may be made of any material which is strong enough to retain the volume of plaster being cast, is not porous, and will easily release from the plaster when it has gone off. Suitable materials for cottling include plastic, wood, lino and soaped plaster slabs. The last can be easily cut and filed to fit the profile of the model. Cottling should be watertight; any small spaces between the cottles should be filled with plastic clay.

A plaster form may be modelled, filed or ground on ground glass to the desired form and texture. If wet plaster is to be poured onto hard plaster in order to effect a join, score the hard plaster to present a rough surface and soak it thoroughly in water. If fresh plaster is to be poured against hard plaster with the intention of dividing the two at a later time, there must be some kind of separator between the two; the most common is soft soap (sometimes called 'potter's size'), which is applied with a sponge kept especially for this purpose. Several coatings should be applied as the first will be absorbed by the plaster.

Three moulds: that at the bottom right contains half of a slip cast.

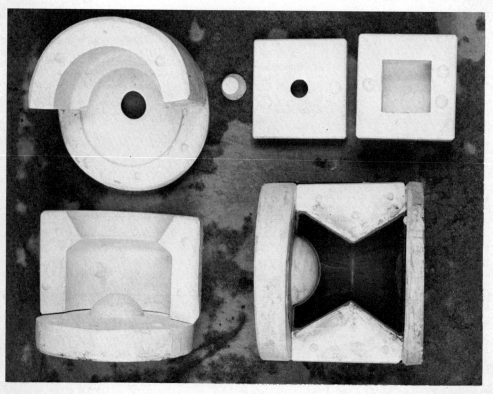

Glazed jugs with wide tops are the most suitable containers in which to mix plaster as they are easy to clean and do not become scratched and contaminated with old plaster. It is important to mix in the proportions advised by the supplier, and avoid contaminating the fresh mix with old, hard plaster, which accelerates the setting reaction. The plaster is always added to the water and in this way an even mix can be fairly easily achieved. When blending plaster avoid whipping air into the mixture, and any lumps should be removed or dissolved. Blending is normally done with the hands but mechanical blenders are used in workshops where large blocks are cast. When drying plaster, do not heat it above 60° C or the plaster will break down and dissolve when it comes into contact with water.

Warning: plaster of paris must not be allowed to contaminate working clay which may be fired. Plaster expands when it absorbs water from the atmosphere. Even a minute particle, finding its way into clay which is then formed and fired, is enough to shear the form if it expands when cool. The result is usually a small crater which appears some time after the form has been fired, thus ruining the piece of work (see page 141).

PLASTER MOULD-MAKING

Tools and materials: coarse file, glazed jug, cottles, modelling tools, soft soap, sponge.

A model may be anything, and made of any material. If special shapes are required they are usually made of plaster, but wood or clay may be used if they are more suited to the form.

Undercuts should be avoided as they may lock the plaster mould to the model. Many objects are available in other materials (especially plastic) which have originally been formed by some moulding process. These usually have the marks of the mould still upon them, which can be guides to indicate where a plaster mould may be divided. All moulds, except those made of clay, should be coated with at least one coat of a suitable separator. Petroleum jelly, thinned with turpentine, and various oils, as well as the more usual soft soap, may be found suitable on different surfaces. The separator should not be so thick that it marks the surface of the model.

The simplest type of mould is a one-piece mould; this will release the model and the cast form without the necessity of divisions in the mould. The type of form possible with this process is inevitably very simple.

The variety of different types of piece mould make it impossible to give any definite rules. The best advice is to start with a two- or three-piece mould and then work up to more complex types. Each piece of the mould must be of equal thickness (usually about two inches), to ensure even

Mould-making. Tinplate is used for the outer cottle, plaster and clay for the side cottle.

casting of the slip, as thick plaster will absorb more water than thin plaster and induce a thicker deposit of clay when used in the casting process. Each piece of the mould is cast separately, usually starting with the top of the form, then each side separately and finally the base. As each piece is cast against the model it should be natched, to provide exact registration of the pieces. Natches are usually in the form of hemispherical depressions (cut with a modelling tool) in the side face of a part of a mould. This produces a hemispherical projection upon the adjacent piece of the mould which is cast against it. Prefabricated natches are commercially available. When the first piece has been cast any rough edges should be cleaned off. Natches must then be made in the sides which will have contact with pieces to be cast later, and the exterior of the mould soaped. Soap must not be allowed to come into contact with the interior surface of the mould as it will destroy the porosity of the surface and render that piece unsuitable for slip casting.

If the mould is designed to cast an enclosed form, a pouring hole must be provided in one of the pieces so that the slip may be poured into and out of the mould. Before pouring that part of the mould it will be necessary to place upon the model a soaped plaster or clay plug, which is removed when the plaster has set hard. This plug should be in the form of a truncated cone with the smaller face in contact with the model. Pouring holes, in the cast, may be filled with small slabs of casting slip but a small hole should be left to allow for the expansion of air within the form as it is fired.

Releasing the model

As the plaster swells during curing, no attempt should be made to remove the model until the plaster is cool. If the model and the several pieces have been adequately coated with separator the mould should release with gentle but sharp tapping. Occasionally levers may have to be used but only with the utmost care, to avoid breaking the mould or the model or both. When the mould has been separated any sharp edges on the outside faces should be removed, in case they break off and combine with the slip during casting (see page 78). The pieces of the mould should then be placed together and clamped either with cord or thick rubber bands (pieces cut from the inner tubes of motor-car tyres are ideal). If cord is used, notches may have to be cut into the outside of the mould to prevent the cord from slipping. If the mould is not clamped during drying and casting there is a danger that it will warp. When the mould has dried out completely – and this may take several days – it is ready to be used for casting.

A complete model and a case mould.

SAND CASTING

The texture of sand upon the cast is an inevitable outcome of this process, which is widely used in industry, particularly in the economical manufacture of complex metal shapes.

Tools and materials: sand-box (a deep, rigid frame of wood or metal with handles on the outside), tamping tool, casting sand (the type used in metal-casting).

Method: place the model on a flat board and the sand-box over it. Pour the sand over the model, ensuring that it fills any narrow recesses. When the sand almost covers the mould, press it down firmly with the tamping tool. Add more sand and tamp it down until the sand reaches the level of the top of the box. Then turn the board and sand-box upside-down, remove the board and lift the model out of the sand. If the sand has enough bonding material it will retain the shape of the model. If the model has any undercuts the moulded sand will tear as it is removed, leaving an imperfect impression.

Casting

If the mould is satisfactory it may be filled with casting slip. The sand is not very absorbent and the slip may take some time to dry to the desired thickness. The sand should be firm enough to withstand being tilted to pour out the excess slip, otherwise the slip must be siphoned from the mould. When it is leather-hard, remove the cast by placing a board across the sand-box and turning it upside-down. The sand is then gently removed from the cast. Obviously to produce a second, similar form the mould must be remade.

More complex moulds may be made but require considerable skill.

The sand casting process.

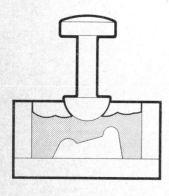
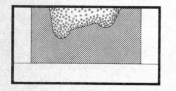

CLAYS FOR SLIP CASTING

The essential qualities of any casting clay is that it should:

1 Cast giving a good definition of the moulded surface.

2 Shrink as little as possible so that moulds need not be unnecessarily large. (Natural clay/water combinations shrink so much from the liquid to the dry state that if they were to be used for slip-casting the mould, for even a small form, would be so large as to be difficult to handle.)

3 Have a satisfactory dry strength.

4 Not wet the mould to such an extent that it has to be dried for long periods between casts.

5 Maintain the clay in suspension and not let it settle to the bottom.

The slip may be of any colour, but not all clays or bodies make good casting slips.

Boots by A Sims, 1971. Height 30 cm. Slip cast, earthenware glaze with platinum lustre.

Robert's Red Wardrobe by D. Hamilton, 1973. Slab built and modelled, with red cadmium glaze.

Deflocculating

This is the name for the practice of adding an electrolyte to the clay so that fluidity may be achieved with the addition of only a small amount of water. Many clays require an equal weight of water to produce a fluid clay/water combination, but a deflocculated slip may contain as little as one quarter of its weight as water and still be suitably liquid. The effect of this is to achieve a slip with low shrinkage from wet to dry and at the same time avoid excessive wetting of the mould. In practice the amount of water which is to make up the slip is weighed out and the correct amount of electrolyte is added to it; this solution is poured into a mixing container and the clay added to it. The best kind of container is a blunger, a large waterproof container with paddles inside it which rotate fairly slowly. Over a period of hours the blunger will mix the water and clay to a smooth liquid.

The exact amount of deflocculant required to produce a satisfactory slip from a given clay may only be determined by experiment, but as a general rule those clays which need more than half of one per cent of their dry weight will be unsuitable for slip casting, as they will probably warp during drying and corrode the plaster mould too quickly. Most suppliers of clays will give advice as to which clays are suitable for casting slips and may specify the amount of deflocculant required.

Too little deflocculant means that the slip will not liquefy without an excessive amount of water; too much will make the slip difficult to trim when cast. Some suppliers will deliver casting slip deflocculated and ready for use in returnable containers.

The most commonly used electrolytes are sodium silicate and soda ash. It is usual to include both these ingredients in equal proportions in a deflocculated slip but this will depend on the clay which is used. There are several different grades of sodium silicate, identified by their potency, measured in 'degrees of twaddle' (° Tw). These grades should not be confused, and the correct type should be used for each clay. Soda ash must be stored in an airtight container as it will combine with airborne water to produce sodium hydroxide; this is a flocculant, and will cause the clay to form lumps and settle as a dense mass on the bottom of the container – a state known as 'livering'.

The effects of electrolytes on clay/water mixtures has not been fully explained, but one theory is that the electrolyte has the effect of reversing the electrical charge of some of the clay particles so that they no longer tend to join together but repel each other to produce a fluid mixture.

Once a satisfactory casting slip has been obtained every effort must be made to preserve its qualities. Any clay which has been dried out and is waste should be discarded or used for some other process but should not be returned to the casting-slip mixture. Waste slip added to good casting

(*Opposite*) *Red X* by John Mason. Height 5 feet. Slab built, with cadmium and selenium glaze.

mixtures can change the qualities of the slip, so rendering the batch useless.

Clay is an abrasive material and alkalis such as sodium silicate and soda ash are corrosive. Together they will wear away a soft material like plaster very quickly. Moulds made of plaster will start to lose sharp edges and definition after several casts have been made. After, say, twenty casts the mould may be so altered as to render it useless. Deflocculated slips will pass some of the electrolyte into the plaster along with the water which is absorbed and in time this will produce a harmless light fur-like growth on the outside of the mould.

Once the mould and the slip have been properly made, the casting of the forms is relatively easy. The slip should be passed through a 120-mesh sieve as it comes from the

A blunger which drains through a vibratory sieve into a container. On the left is a mixer for blending slips and glazes.

Filling case moulds; that on the right is ready to be topped up as the level of the slip has fallen below the top of the mould.

blunger and sieved again before use if it has been stored. The smooth slip is then poured into the mould until it is full and topped up during the casting time. Failure to do this may lead to inaccurate measuring of the cast thickness, and thick sections in the lower half of the cast. As the slip lies in the mould, water is absorbed by those surfaces of the plaster which are in contact with it, the effect of which is to produce a layer of clay at this point. As more water is absorbed by the plaster a thicker layer of clay will be formed, until either the mould becomes saturated with water or the layer of clay becomes so dense that water will no longer pass through it. In practice the slip and the mould are so designed that neither of these situations occurs before the cast is of the desired thickness.

Draining the mould.

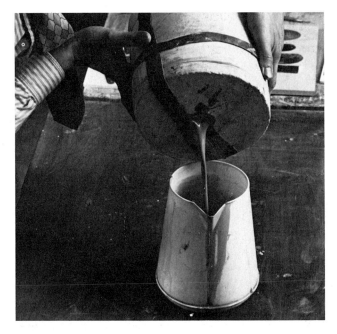

The time taken pouring the slip into the mould, until it has cast the desired thickness, is termed the 'casting time'. The easiest way to test the thickness of the cast at any point during the casting time is to tilt the mould so that the thickness of the layer of slip may be seen adhering to the wall of the mould.

When the cast has achieved the correct thickness the mould may be turned upside-down over a bowl or bucket so that the excess slip drains out, leaving a hollow cast. When draining the mould, ensure that no pieces of plaster fall from the mould into the casting slip. Plaster of paris is a flocculant causing the clay in the casting slip to settle out.

When the cast form within the mould has lost its shiny surface, trim it with a sharp knife, taking care not to pull the clay away from the mould as this will distort the form. Upon reaching the leather-hard state of drying the mould may be opened and the cast removed. At this stage pare away with a knife, discard any 'spares' that were necessary in the casting process, and smooth off any rough edges with a damp sponge. If the form is such that it must be made in several pieces, or modelled or changed in any way, this must be done at the leather-hard stage. Cast forms may be joined one to the other in a dry state but this is a hazardous procedure for a novice, as the forms are very fragile. Cross-hatching before joining two cast forms is not always necessary and either casting slip or water may be used to effect a satisfactory union.

Cast forms dry quickly and after twenty-four hours should be ready for the first firing.

The mould, the unfettled cast and a fired cast (note the shrinkage).

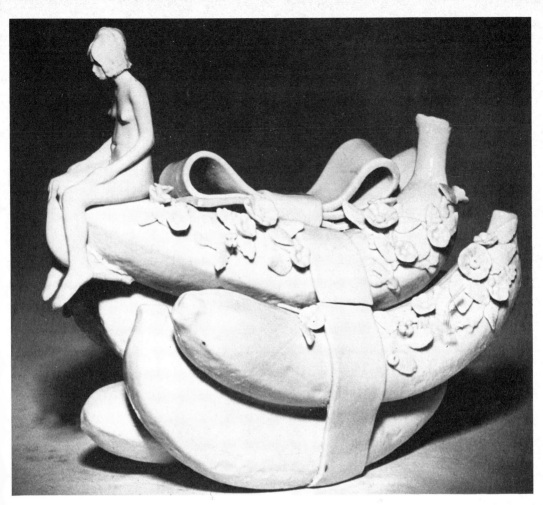

Figure with bananas by Jack Earl,
1968. Covered jar, slip-cast and
modelled in porcelain.

Landscape bowl by Irene Sims.
Semi-porcelain, slip-cast and
modelled with airbrushed colour
under the glaze.

9 Machine methods of forming clay

The direct application of the information in this chapter will inevitably depend on the availability of equipment. Although there are many variations in the detailed design of different makes of equipment, all tend to conform to basic principles. In general, new equipment is developed to increase specialized output where hand or skilled processes have become uneconomic. Two of the three methods outlined represent those which might be available in a studio workshop and may be used without much practice. The other process is that known as 'throwing' and is probably the most popular and attractive process to the novice.

THROWING

The ability to 'throw' a clay form on a wheel will require considerable patience and practice. There is no one way to throw. The process has been used at least since the third millennium B C, and has inevitably been subject to the variations of differing cultures and ages. Thrown forms may fairly be said to reveal as much about the maker as would his handwriting. Therefore, while idiosyncrasies are not sought in the process, each thrower will develop his or her characteristics. Once the skill has been acquired it is a very rapid method of forming clay and is the commonest technique in studio potteries. Although the process of throwing tends to produce round forms it is nevertheless capable of many variations of form.

Wheels

Wheels are of several types, driven either by the thrower or a motor. The usual manual wheel is driven either by kicking the flywheel or moving a crank lever attached to the spindle. In the Orient, wheels may be driven by spinning the flywheel by hand, then throwing until the wheel has lost momentum and then spinning it again. Mechanical wheels are usually driven by an electric motor through various friction drives or a variable rheostat. There are several schools of thought on the subject of wheels and the virtues of kick-wheels as against electric wheels. This is a personal matter and the only advice to be offered is that

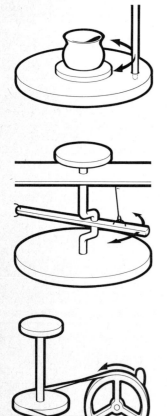

Manual throwing wheels: (*top*), oriental wheel; (*middle*), kick wheel; (*bottom*), belt-driven wheel (the driving wheel is turned manually).

both types should be tried and, if possible, varieties of each type.

Types of clay

Clays for throwing should be plastic and not too fine or they will become slimy during the throwing process. Many surface clays are quite suitable for throwing once they have been cleaned of any stones or vegetable matter. Purpose-made bodies are available from suppliers. Fireclays are usually too coarse to be used for throwing but can be used if protective pads of leather are fastened to the fingers and palms of the hands. Porcelain and bone china can be thrown only with difficulty as they have a puttyish feel and tend to collapse unless thrown thicker than the final desired section, in which case the complete form must be turned to the desired thickness when leather-hard.

Wedging

First, the clay must be wedged until it is a homogeneous mass with no foreign bodies or air bubbles. There are two methods of wedging.

Tools: cutting wire or harp, wedging bench or solid table.

Method: the first involves kneading in a manner rather like kneading bread. This is difficult to explain in detail except to say that the motion is a spiral turning, twisting and pressing all in one movement. The second method is easier to explain and probably easier for the novice to master. Form the clay into a wedge-shaped block, the thumbs of both hands placed on the left-hand side so that the fingers are spread over the edge of the clay. Then lift up the wedge and turn it through ninety degrees so that it comes down with the face which was on the left now on the top. With the cutting wire or harp cut the clay parallel to the working surface. Remove the top piece and smooth out the cut surface of the piece remaining on the bench, being sure to remove any foreign matter and to squeeze out any air bubbles. By patting the surface with the palms of the hands it should be formed into a gentle, smooth curve. The top piece is then taken and similarly treated except that the cut surface is kept flat. Next, lift up the top piece with the palms of the hands on the side opposite that which has been cut, and smack it down on to the curved top of the lower piece. A loud crack may be heard as the air is violently expelled from between the two pieces. There must be no indentations in either of the two meeting surfaces as these will trap air, and air bubbles in the clay can make throwing the clay difficult and may cause the clay to 'bloat' during firing. This process is repeated ten or twelve times, each cut being at ninety degrees to the previous one by virtue of the process of turning the clay over. The mass of clay is finally cut into

Powered throwing wheels: (*top*), wheel friction drive; (*middle*), double cone wheel; (*bottom*), variable-speed d.c. motor wheel.

Wedging

Two coloured clays are used to illustrate the process.

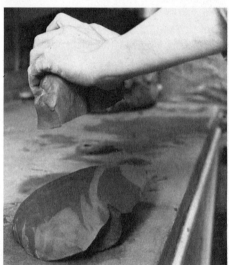

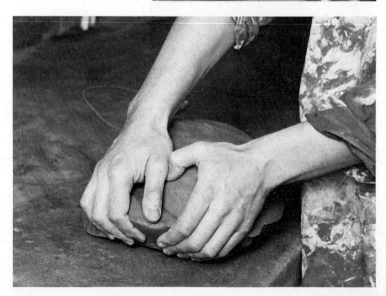

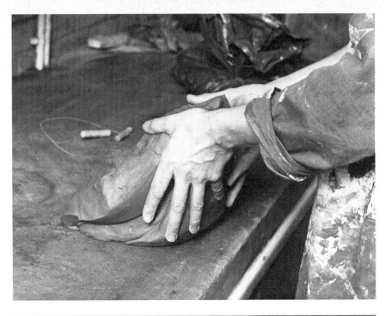

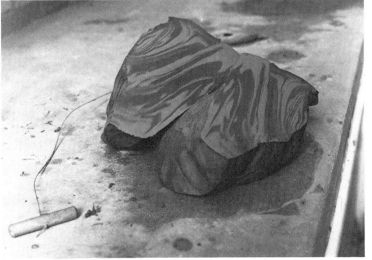

Half-wedged clay.

Completed wedging
and ball-making.

pieces of suitable weight, which are then patted into balls ready to be thrown.

Tools for throwing: wheel, cutting wire, natural sponge, turning tools, needle, bowl of water.

Method: there are several principles involved in the process of throwing. The spinning action of the wheel will tend to throw the clay upwards and outwards once the mass of clay has been hollowed out. If the initial hollowing out is not carefully carried out more clay may rise on one side than the other, causing the clay to wobble uncontrollably. The three main procedures are:

1 Centring – moving the clay onto the centre of the wheel and then ensuring that it is spinning as a homogeneous mass round the axis.

2 Hollowing out – determining the depth of clay to remain as the base of the form (usually about three-quarters of an inch to one inch), and the shape and size of the interior base.

3 Raising – squeezing the clay walls to give the desired height and making the final form.

Throughout these processes the wheel is used to increase the forces acting upon the clay. Therefore maximum speed may be used to centre and hollow out the clay. But the wider, higher or thinner the form becomes, the slower the wheel should run.

Water is used as a lubricant between hands and clay, throughout throwing. In time the clay will become saturated with water and will collapse, so there is a time limit of between five and ten minutes to form the clay once it has been entered.

Centring: note the position of the left arm.

Centring

Clean the wheel-head of any clay and dampen it with water.
Place a ball of clay on the centre of the wheel and press it
down so that it sticks firmly to the wheel. Centre the clay
at first by steadying it with both hands while spinning the
wheel. To keep both hands firm and to minimize the effort
involved, tuck the elbow of the left arm into the hip and
lean the whole body forward; in this way sufficient force
may be exerted through the forearm and the palm of the
hand. The principle is that the force should be transmitted
through the bone while the muscles are relaxed, so that
fatigue is avoided. Inexperienced potters tend to stiffen the
fingers while centring and this can cause cramp as well as
wasting energy. If the clay comes off the wheel-head or
starts to slide it usually means either (1) there is too much
water beneath the clay, or (2) the clay is too wet for the
force acting on it, or (3) the clay has not been pressed firmly
onto the wheel.

When the clay is in the centre of the wheel it is ready for
coning. Place the forearms upon the side of the tray round the
wheel with the elbows wide apart, both hands round the
spinning clay, so that the lower part of the palms and balls of
the thumbs are opposite each other. By levering the elbows
inwards force can be exerted upon the clay to squeeze it
upwards. As the clay is raised it should be steadied with the
hands. If the clay starts to rise above the level of the top of
the hands, raise the hands simultaneously so that the top of
the clay is always in contact with the thumbs. Once the clay
has been raised to a slender cone, remove the hands slowly
and gently. Any sudden pressure will force the clay off
centre, and equally sudden release of pressure will allow the
clay to spring back and go off centre.

Coning: a front view demonstrating
the correct arm and hand positions.

Coning (side view).

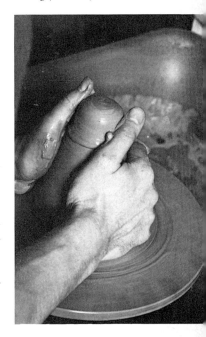

85

Compressing the cone.

The clay on centre.

Hollowing out the clay
with the thumb.

86

Now change the position of the hands so that the left hand runs against the left side of the top of the cone while the right hand is placed, palm down, upon the top. The fingers of the right hand will then overlap the back of the left hand. By moving the right shoulder towards the clay and simultaneously pressing downwards, the clay can be compressed with relative ease. The left hand serves to steady the clay and, by maintaining steady pressure, forms the clay into a truncated cone.

All these procedures are carried out with the palms of the hands; the fingers should not be used as they tend to form ridges in the clay, which may prove difficult to remove later.

The coning should be repeated four or five times, and when finally pressed down the clay should be running smoothly on perfect centre.

Hollowing out

Once the clay has been centred, place the hands round the clay with the thumbs on top. Press the right-hand thumb into the centre of the clay to form a hollow, the depth of which should be such that about one inch of clay remains between the thumb and the wheel-head. The hollow is then widened as required by moving the thumb to the right. As the clay is widened so the speed of the wheel should be reduced. The bottom of the hollow should be perfected – and should be flat for a tall form or curved for a bowl form – before proceeding.

Raising

To raise the walls, place the left hand in the hollow and the right hand outside; if the form is small enough the two thumbs may be interlocked. The elbows should be tucked well into the body to improve control. If pressure is exerted

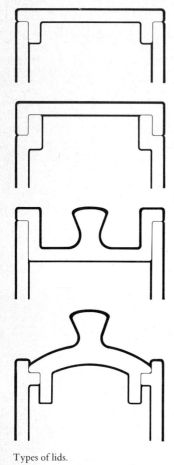

Types of lids.

through the fingers, which should be opposite each other at the quarter past three position of the spinning clay, the wall of the clay will rise. As the wall rises, let the hands rise with it so that the point of pressure gradually moves up the clay form. As the clay becomes taller, so the speed of the wheel should be decreased.

Once the first raising action is complete, the fingers return to the base of the clay, and with renewed pressure the clay will rise further. Several pulls may be necessary to achieve the desired height. Too much pressure will produce lines of weakness in the form and it will collapse; too little pressure will fail to raise the clay. Generally, more pressure (and faster spinning of the wheel) will be required when working on the lower and thicker parts of the clay form. The top third is usually the weakest and softest part so pressure should be very gently applied. It is usual to stop the hands one eighth of an inch below the top of the clay to avoid the fingers slipping across the top edge and bending it.

Particular attention should be paid to the top edge of the form. If it is uneven it may be trimmed by placing a needle through the wall about half an inch below the top, spinning the wheel and removing the cut piece. The cut edge is, however, usually considered incompatible with the thrown form and is softened by gentle sponging while the clay is spinning.

Centring, coning and hollowing out should be practised until the clay can be controlled with ease. To test the quality of the throwing, cut the practice piece in half with a cutting wire. The section should be thick at the bottom, tapering to about halfway, and then become even up to the lip of the form. -

As the clay is wet and soft when thrown, it is necessary to leave sufficient clay at the bottom of the wall to support the raised clay. This is removed by turning (see page 92).

To throw a straight-sided cylinder, the tendency of the clay to expand outwards must be constantly corrected. In the forming of a curved bowl shape this tendency will be helpful.

In all throwing, the inside shape is formed and the outer shape, while not being ignored, should not be the sole criterion. This will demand a conscious effort on the part of the beginner.

Small objects (up to six inches high and four inches wide) should be attempted first, and once these have been mastered the novice may progress to larger shapes. The maximum weight which most mechanical wheels will throw is about thirty pounds. The maximum weight for kick-wheels will depend on the design of the wheel and the skill and strength of the thrower.

When the form has been thrown it must be removed by cutting through the base as near to the wheel-head as possible with a cutting wire. First, sponge any water from the interior, pare away the excess clay from the bottom of the form

Completing the
cylindrical form.

Completing the bowl
form.

A recessed lid.

89

A spout or small bottle.

Another type of thrown lid.

Pulling the spout of a jug.

90

and run water onto the wheel-head with a sponge. Grasp the cutting wire in both hands with the thumbs on the wire itself so that as the wire is pushed from the front of the wheel-head through the clay, the thumbs press the wire onto the wheel and prevent it from rising up and cutting the bottom out of the clay form. The wire should be passed through the clay several times, ensuring that plenty of water is pushed between the clay and the wheel-head. After this the clay should be eased across the wheel onto a suitable bat and placed to dry.

(*Top*) Cleaning the base of a thrown form.

(*Above*) Cutting the form from the wheel.

Turning

As soon as the top of the form is firm it should be turned over
onto a clean surface so that the base may stiffen. When the
base is leather-hard, the form should be put upside-down
on a clean wheel and centred by slowly turning the wheel
and pushing the form gently to the exact centre on which it
was thrown. (It is wise to feel the thickness of the sides and
base and make a note of the quantity of clay to be turned off,
before placing the form on the wheel.) When this has been
achieved (and it requires patience for the first few times) a
coil of clay should be placed round the outside of the clay
against the wheel and pressed down, while ensuring that the
form is not moved or pressed out of shape. The clay is
pared off with a turning tool of which there are several
types. Usually the base is turned true by cutting concentric
circles to a constant depth and then cutting across these from
the centre outwards, to the depth of the rings. Take care
that the base of the form is not cut out by accident.

After the base has been turned, treat the sides in the same
way, being careful not to turn off too much. The foot of
a pot is turned when the base is being turned, but ensure
that the foot is higher than the centre of the base as, if not,
the finished form will rock. The final section of the form
should be even through the base and walls. But large forms
may require extra clay support at the bottom of the wall.
If the base is flat, press it until it is slightly curved, so that
stresses set up during drying and firing do not cause it to
split.

Additions to clay forms

There may be occasions when it is desired to join pieces of
clay formed by other processes to a thrown form. This is
usually done when it is in the leather-hard state, and all the
rules of hand-modelling processes will apply.

Fixing the form to the wheel before
turning.

Cutting the rings in the base of a form.

Levelling off the base.

Cutting away the excess clay from the sides of a form.

93

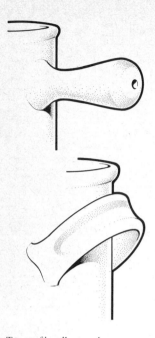

Handles are not usually modelled or cast if they are to be applied to a thrown form. The processes of extruding or 'pulling' are preferable as they produce a surface more compatible with that of throwing. Extrusion is dealt with below, and pulled handles on page 64. The only variation relevant here is the making of a wire tool, rather like a wire modelling tool but shaped to the profile of the handle section. Drawn through a block of clay, such a tool will produce a shaped strip which may be formed into a handle.

It is advisable to pull several handles for each form at first, of various types, thickness, width and length so that the most suitable handle for the form in question can be chosen.

Types of handle: *top*, thrown; *bottom*, pulled.

Extruding

A hand-driven, motorized pugmill or a wad-box is necessary if it is desired to extrude clay forms. A wad-box can be thought of as a cartridge of clay which is forced through a die. A pugmill resembles an enlarged household mincing-machine which drives the clay down a threaded central column and through a die. A de-airing pugmill includes a vacuum chamber to remove any air and increase the plasticity of the clay. In this process the clay is forced through a die which has been cut to the shape of the section required for the clay extrusion. Pressure must be sufficient to force the clay through the die, and the clay must be in such a state that it will not tear or crack. In the case of hollow or large extrusions a de-airing pugmill is necessary to remove air pockets and to ensure a dense and even extrusion. Laminations, caused by the rotary action of the augers, may occur in extruded forms and these may cause the form to crack when dried and fired.

Most clay drainpipes are made by extruding clay, as are the ceramic cores for various electric appliances, including

A de-airing pugmill extruding a square-section tube.

electric fires. Tubular kiln props are also made by this technique. Eighteenth- and nineteenth-century handles for jugs and tea- and coffee-pots were extruded through dies in a wad-box.

Method: the shape of the die should be decided upon, and cut through a piece of metal which will not flex excessively. If the shape is simple then the die may be made of wood. All dies should have the inside edge bevelled so that the clay is compressed through the die and shaped finally by the outer face. If the form is to be a hollow tube a two-piece die will be necessary (internal and external). The inner die is usually fixed to a removable back plate in such a manner that it projects forward, with its end flush with the face of the external die. These dies normally need to be made from steel and require precision engineering. Carefully set up, they will produce a tube with walls of even thickness throughout. Manufacturers of dies will produce them to specification but these are expensive and economical only for long production runs.

Once the dies are fixed in place the clay is fed into the pugmill or wad-box and the pressure applied either with the motor or by turning the handle. As the extruded clay comes out it may be of such a shape that it will not support itself. If so, make a support and let the piece extrude onto it. In any case it will be necessary to extrude onto a movable board which will allow the clay to slide as it is pushed out by the pugmill. With a wad-box, the clay is usually extruded

(Left, above) Vertical pugmill: the hopper has a pressure feed lever.

(Right, above) A de-airing pugmill with three sets of dies for producing hollow tubes.

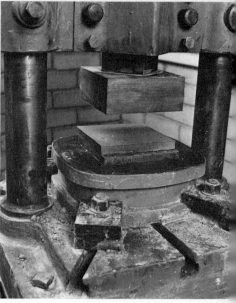

(*Above*) Filling and levelling off the dies of a fly press.

(*Above, right*) A pressed tile, raised by means of the lower die, in the process of being removed.

vertically so that it comes out of the bottom and can be cut off in the appropriate lengths and laid carefully on a board.

DUST AND PLASTIC PRESSING

A fly or hand press is necessary for the pressing of dust clay and is desirable with plastic clay pressing. The procedure may be briefly described as the bonding together of dry clay, in shaped dies, under great pressure so that the tile is strong enough to hold together until fired. For dry pressing the water content is kept down to between 5 and 15 per cent, this being sufficient to bond the particles of clay.

Many non-conducting electrical porcelains are dry-pressed, as are all industrial tiles. As the water content is very low there is very little warpage during drying so that the tiles retain their shape and may be fired quickly.

The dies for pressing are made from steel for long runs but wood or soft metal can be used for short runs.

Method: once the shape and pattern or texture of the dies has been decided upon and the dies made (both a die for the top of the tile and one for the bottom) place them in the press and fill the bottom die with a measured amount of clay. (The exact amount of clay necessary to produce a tile of the desired thickness must be determined by experiment.) Apply the pressure and then release it, remove the compressed piece and set it to dry. If dust or plastic clay sticks to the die, first inspect the surface of the die to ensure that there are no undercuts which are locking the piece. If this is not the cause then the clay is too wet and should be dried out. If this is undesirable, the die must be treated with a water repellent such as rape-seed oil, and this coating regularly reapplied as necessary.

Two tiles and the die plates which were produced by etching with acid.

(*Left*) A hand-operated fly press.

10 Changing the surface before bisquit firing

Any clay form may have properties, either inherent or induced by the forming process, which may be completely satisfying without even a glaze. Nevertheless there is a range of techniques which can enrich the surface in graphic or plastic ways. These techniques can be used to clarify the meaning of a piece of work, and until the invention of white opaque glazes they were the most commonly used methods of decorating the surface of ceramic forms (see page 122).

MODELLING

For a list of suitable tools see pages 47 to 51.

As the clay remains in a plastic state for some time after it has been formed it is natural during this period to consider the possibilities of modelling or texturing the surface. If there are any irregularities in the form, modelling the surface may well camouflage them.

One type of modelling involves the removal of some of the clay with a modelling tool, knife, flute or sharp stick. These cuts may be directional to create a linear force, or random to create a texture. If the lines are directional then lines running round a form will tend to emphasize the girth and if vertical the lines will exaggerate the height. Lines or grooves cut at an angle of forty-five degrees to the vertical are traditionally favoured for pottery as such marks will draw the attention to the roundness of the form without making it appear unduly squat. Grooves, lines or various stippled textures are sometimes combined, with pleasing effect. Certain types of glaze will produce rich surfaces over forms treated in this way (see Chapter 14). Incised lines and textures can be filled with coloured engobes or colouring oxides (see Chapter 11). It is also possible to make indentations in the surface by pressing textured objects against the form – natural materials such as grass or tree bark, man-made such as fabric, screws etc., or special stamps made for this process. Potters' stamps, used to mark objects with the maker's mark or a name, are used at this stage.

Building up parts of the surface with pieces of clay presents no problems provided that the applied clay is at the same state of dryness (preferably leather-hard) as the form; the two clays should also be of similar thermal expansion. The

Large ceramic horse, 78 cm. high. T'ang Dynasty.

colour of the applied clay may be changed (see page 29) and it can also be modelled before it is applied (modelled clay additions to a form are called 'sprigs'). It may be necessary to cross-hatch and slurry the area of the form to which the sprig is to be applied.

Cut, impressed or applied marks may lose definition under thick glazes, and experiments should be undertaken to test the compatibility of glaze and modelled texture.

COLOURING

The following items will be necessary if the methods of applying colours are to be explored.

Brushes. There are many different types of brush; some have quite specific qualities and uses, and others may be considered as 'general-purpose' brushes. All brushes are subjected to considerable wear when used to paint on clay, so regular replacement is essential for good-quality work.

Sable brushes, sold as artists' brushes, are useful as substitutes for many of the more specialized types. They are expensive but carry colouring solutions well.

Majolica pencils, which can be bought as hair fixed to ferrules so that they may be fitted to a handle of the painter's choice, are designed for painting on unfired dry glaze. Very fine work is possible when using these.

Cut liners are designed to lay on bands of colour. The thickness of the lines will depend on the thickness and cut of the hair.

Glaze mops are large fat brushes which will carry a lot of glaze solution when painting glaze on a form.

Japanese brushes come in a variety of shapes and sizes but are less springy than sable brushes. Ideal for calligraphic work and free brushwork, they are designed to be used for painting gestural marks. It is more difficult to use them for fine, controlled painting.

Wax resist brushes. Hog-hair brushes are suitable as they have the firmness which wax resist painting often requires, and they should never be used for anything other than wax solutions.

Always wash brushes in clean water after use and place them in a box or hang them up. If they are placed in a box, their hairs should be protected with a paper tube to hold them together. Careful storage will do much to lengthen the life of an expensive brush. It is advisable to keep separate brushes for painting enamels which have been mixed with oil media as it is very difficult to remove all the oil from such brushes. Non-ferrous or quill ferrules are best suited for ceramic use as there is no danger of corrosion of the ferrule, which can produce unwanted iron contamination of the colours.

(*Opposite, above*) *The Agony in the Garden,* altarpiece in glazed terracotta relief by Andrea della Robbia (1435–1525).

(*Opposite*) Slipware dish signed by Thomas Toft (*c.* 1680).

(*Above*, *left*) Peruvian annular vessel with stirrup spout. Hand-built and modelled.

(*Above and left*) Medieval English jugs, thrown and cut from the wheel without turning the base. Modelled surfaces, galena (lead ore) glazed.

Combs, made from wood, metal or plastic, when drawn across a coloured ground will produce a series of parallel lines. Pieces of hacksaw blade will produce similar effects.

Slip trailers. Rubber bulbs or reservoirs with fine nozzle outlets are the common form of 'slip trailers'. As the name implies, a slip trailer is a trailing instrument rather like a cake icer. The reservoir is filled with an engobe and then gently squeezed to produce a trail of engobe upon the clay surface. Nozzles of different sizes are required, as are several bulbs if different-coloured slips are to be used simultaneously. Always wash out the nozzle and bulb after use, otherwise the slip will dry out and leave behind a hard mass of clay which takes a long time to become liquid again even if left to soak in water.

Stencils. A stencil may be considered to be anything with holes in it, through which a colour may be sprayed. Sieves, colanders, perforated metal can all be used. Paper may be cut to a similar pattern and is commonly used to resist areas of clay when a form is to be coated with an engobe (see page 110). Paper of the kind which is shiny on one side and matt on the other should be ideal in its absorbent quality and wet strength. Paper stencils should be damped to make them elastic and adhere to the clay. Care must be exercised when removing stencils which are in contact with the clay surface if damage to the edge of the coloured shape is to be avoided.

Wax resist. Traditionally, wax with a little turpentine was used for painting wax on clay. This is heated until it is liquid and is painted on the form with a brush kept for this purpose only. It cools rapidly and forms a waterproof surface which will resist any colour or water-mixed glaze applied to the rest of the form. Wax emulsions are now commercially available but have a different quality from true wax. Emulsions are convenient to use and are easily cleaned from brushes which are washed in water. Both types of wax burn away during the firing to reveal the surface beneath.

PAINTING

Painting on an unfired clay surface should be undertaken when the clay is drier than if it were to be modelled. At the drier stage the pigment can be suspended in water to make a thin solution about the strength of watercolour. This is then applied to the clay, which will absorb the water and leave the pigment on the surface. It is important to use restraint when applying metal oxides as they are very strong colorants. Every brush-stroke will show in the finished glazed state so the pigment must be applied with care: it is almost impossible to erase a painted mark. Even if it seems to have been cleaned away some of the colour will almost certainly develop in the glaze. This may be seen initially as a handicap

but it can lead to a spontaneous type of image when practice
has bred confidence.

Manufactured 'underglaze colours' are mixtured of colouring oxides carefully compounded to produce standardized
colours. This may be an advantage or a disadvantage
according to the type of image being created, These colours
should always be applied according to the manufacturers'
instructions.

Resists. Stencils may be used to mask out those areas which
are not to be coloured. Paper stencils should be absorbent
so that when damped with water they will adhere to the dry
clay form.

Spraying. Pigments may be applied by means of an aerograph. There will be no texture in the appearance of the
coloured ground and with practice it is possible to produce
graded colours.

Banding. Stripes or bands of colour may be painted on
circular forms by centring them on a banding wheel and
holding a loaded brush so that it deposits a line of colour as
the form is spun round.

Engobes may be applied to clay forms before bisquit
firing (see next chapter).

11 Engobes

An engobe is a solution of clay and water which is applied to a clay form, usually in order to change the colour of all or part of the form. An engobe used in this way can be likened to a veneer. In some cases the engobe is used for technical reasons but normally the intention is to achieve a decorative effect.

There is occasionally some confusion over the proper use of the terms 'engobe' and 'slip'. Both are solutions of clay and water but the word 'engobe' is used specifically to describe a coat of slip applied to a clay form, whereas a slip may be used to make the form itself in the manufacturing process called 'slip casting' (see page 67). All engobes are slips but not all slips are engobes.

The use of engobes was probably one of man's first conscious acts of colouring clay vessels. It would be a natural development of the discovery of deposits of secondary clays with differing impurities and fired colours. The attraction of engobes to many ceramists is the similarity between the composition of engobes and clay bodies, which makes them easy to use, and the rich, subtle, natural colours together with the feeling of technical and aesthetic compatibility of the materials. Some of the finest ceramics using engobes demonstrate a richness and spontaneity difficult to achieve with other materials.

Flat clay slabs prepared and decorated using any of the following techniques may be dried to a leather-hard state and formed by the methods discussed in Chapter 7.

QUALITIES

As clay is the basic ingredient, engobes are always opaque unless the application is very thin. They can be coloured to almost any hue or tone but traditionally the colours chosen reflect the earthy nature of clay. The fired surface of an engobe can be likened to a dense, opaque, underfired glaze, and as with glazes it is essential that the engobe fit the clay body to which it is applied. To this end, it must be applied while the body is in a 'green' or leather-hard state, so that body and engobe may shrink at the same rate. If it is necessary to apply the engobe to a dry or bisquited form then it must be made up so that its shrinkage is limited (see formula below). An engobe formulated for bisquit fit may be very similar to a matt glaze; it may indeed be vitrified and therefore have some of the properties of a glaze surface. At earthenware temperatures the type of glaze, either alkaline or basic, will affect the final colour (see page 146). When fired in conjunction with matt stoneware glazes, some engobes, particularly those with a high proportion (8 per cent) of metal oxides, tend to boil up through the glaze, often giving a rich, textured result.

Engobes may be textured by the addition of grog, fireclay or a similar finely ground material which will withstand the firing temperature; such textured engobes are unsuitable for tableware as they create a surface unsympathetic to handling or cleaning.

The essential qualities of an engobe are three: (1) it must shrink during drying at the same rate as the form to which it is applied; (2) it must expand and contract at the same rate as the form during the firing cycle; (3) it must be of the desired colour and texture.

To ensure that conditions (1) and (2) are met, the engobe should be made from the same clay as the form. If this is not possible or desirable then experiment will be needed to determine whether or not the correct fit has been achieved.

For application to greenware, the engobe may be anything from 100 per cent clay to equal parts of clay, china clay and flint; exact proportions must be determined by experiment.

For application to dry or bisquit earthenware: one part each of calcined china clay, clay, flint, borax frit.

For dry or bisquit stoneware: one part each of calcined china clay, clay, flint, felspar.

If an engobe peels, increase the proportion of ball clay, or use uncalcined china clay; if it crazes, increase the proportions of calcined china clay and flint.

APPLICATION

Before applying an engobe, ensure that the clay form is structurally suitable. In the application of any engobe, water is conveyed to the clay object, and if this is thin or structurally weak there is a danger that the absorbed water will weaken the clay to the point of collapse. In the case of hollow shapes which are to be coated inside and out it is usual to apply the engobe to the inside before turning or cutting the form to its final section thickness. Large bowls normally have any engobe applied to the inside and are then allowed to dry again to a leather-hard state.

Handles on cups and jugs are prone to collapse if covered with engobe. Great care must be taken in the design of the handle, application of the engobe and drying of the form to avoid the loss of many hours' work. This problem does not occur when applying an engobe to a bisquited object. The engobe, in a working condition, is usually a half-and-

Slip-trailed engobe patterns.

half solution of clay material and water, but a more reliable guide is that it should be the consistency of single (thin) cream.

In most methods of engobe application, if the design is found unsuitable or marred in some way the engobe may be removed with a soft sponge, which must be cleaned regularly in water. It is advisable to let the clay dry a little before repeating the procedure as water absorption may cause the form to collapse.

Dipping

Make up the engobe and sieve it through an 80-mesh sieve into a container; this should be of such proportions that the object may, if necessary, be totally immersed in the solution and then withdrawn, the excess solution being allowed to drain away before the object is placed to dry.

Hollow objects are usually one-third filled with engobe, and the form tilted to an angle of forty-five degrees so that the slip coats the inside as the form is rotated. After drying, the outside can be coated by dipping it upside-down into the solution and allowing the air pressure within the form to prevent the engobe entering inside it. In this way engobes of different colours may be applied to the inner and outer surfaces.

'Window dipping' is a term used to describe the partial immersion of the side of the object in the engobe solution.

Trailing

This technique is similar to that of icing a cake. The engobe solution, which should be the consistency of double (thick)

(*Opposite, above*) Feathered and
finger-drawn engobe patterns.

(*Above*) Anglo-Roman beaker: a
thrown and turned form with slip-
trailed images in similar clay,
unglazed.

cream, is forced from a reservoir or slip trailer through a
fine nozzle onto the clay form, and as the nozzle is moved over
the surface of the form it deposits a raised line of slip. Take
care, when drawing the engobe across a vertical surface, to
avoid undesirable runs or dribbles. The consistency of the
engobe is critical: too thick a mixture will be difficult to
force continuously through the nozzle and too thin a mixture
will flow uncontrollably over the clay form. Sieve the mixture to remove lumps, which might cause a blockage in the
nozzle. Skill is needed to achieve fine and intricate results:
practise on a clean plaster slab before attempting anything
other than the simplest of images.

The final image is raised slightly above the level of the clay
form and can usually be felt as an undulating surface even
when covered with a glaze (see page 100, lower picture).

Feathering

Feathering is a process related to slip trailing. The clay
form (usually flat) should be covered with a layer of thin
engobe. While this layer is still wet, trail a thicker engobe
of a different colour in parallel lines over the surface. If the
clay is a flat surface and supported by a board it can be
knocked by bumping it up and down so that the thicker
engobe drops into the thinner, and the thicker slip appears as
very thin and delicate lines. Prepare a feather (a goose
feather is often best suited to this technique) by stripping off
the hairs at the narrow end to leave a thin tapering spine,
which is very flexible. If this spine is drawn at right angles
across the parallel lines of thicker engobe it will pull them
very slightly in the direction in which the feather is moved.

(*Opposite*) Slipware dish by Charles
Vyse, 1936; diameter 19 cm.
Feathered slip on buff clay, press-
moulded over a hump mould; transparent stoneware glaze.

108

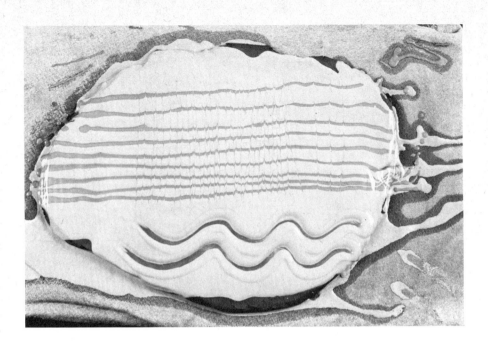

Detail of marbled slip border on a press-moulded dish.

Marbling

Cover the clay form in thin engobe, and then pour engobe of another colour over part of it. When the form is spun or shaken, the engobes flow over the clay to produce a surface similar in quality to the markings in marble. This is a somewhat chancy procedure and several attempts may be necessary before a satisfactory result is achieved.

Encaustic

The clay form (often a tile) is made with recesses, either moulded or modelled, which are flooded with engobe. When the engobe is leather-hard or quite dry, the surface of the form is cleaned back to reveal the original clay surface with the recesses filled with engobe. This method starts with a relief form the colour of the body and ends with a flat, coloured surface. With tiles, this creates a permanent image which is still evident after considerable wear. On a textured surface, encaustic serves to heighten the texture by giving it a colour contrast.

Stencil

Stencils may be cut from paper, moistened with water to soften them and placed against the clay object. The engobe can then be poured, sprayed or painted over the surface and when it is leather-hard the stencil can be removed.

Wax resist

Marbled engobe patterns.

Wax or wax emulsion can be painted on the clay; the engobe is then poured over the surface and will run off those areas

Medieval encaustic floor tiles (thirteenth century) from the cloister of Titchfield Abbey, Hampshire.

Sudanese figure of a hyena, twentieth century. Hand-built and modelled, with a textured surface filled with contrasting engobe.

Sphere and bowl by Irene Sims, slip-cast with stencilled vitrifying engobe applied to the bisquit. The sphere is unglazed.

which have been coated with wax. If the engobe is sprayed over wax the atomized particles tend to adhere to the wax.

Sgraffito

When the engobe is applied to the clay form, parts of it can be removed, by drawing or scratching with a sharp wooden stick or bamboo, to reveal the clay beneath it. Very fine results can be achieved by this method, the quality of line varying with the type of drawing-stick which is used and the state of dryness of the engobe and clay body.

The reverse procedure is also frequently used, in which the surface of the clay is scratched and the incised line flooded with engobe. When dry the form is scraped clean to reveal the precise line as drawn.

Terra sigillata

Terra sigillata is a type of engobe commonly found on Roman and Greek pottery. It is characterized by a burnished surface and is usually red-brown or black in colour. The engobe consists of very fine particles of clay which are gathered by mixing clay with water to make a thin solution, allowing it to stand for two or three days and then decanting the surface water. The top third only of the remaining solution is siphoned off, and applied to the ware. It may be burnished with a polished tool to increase the shine, but should not be fired above 950° C as the polish will start to fade above this temperature.

Chinese jar of Tz'u Chou ware, Yüan Dynasty. Thrown form, slip-glazed with sgraffito design.

A jar by the Martin brothers, late nineteenth century. Thrown form painted with thin blue slip, the sgraffito image filled with iron oxide. Transparent stoneware glaze fired in a salt-glaze firing.

12 Drying and firing

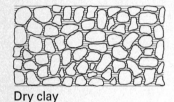

Dry clay

Wet clay

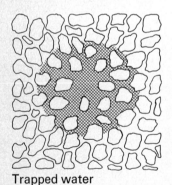

Trapped water

Water in clay.

Any working clay will contain water. The water is present in two forms: free water, which lies between the particles of clay; combined water, which helps to make up the particles of clay.

If the clay is left exposed to air at room temperature it will start to dry, which is shown by its becoming harder and lighter in colour. What actually happens is that the water is drawn into the air by evaporation. If the clay is to be kept damp it must remain surrounded by damp air, so it can be seen that the condition of the air is critical to the drying process. If the clay object is placed in warm air it will become even drier as warm air carries more water than cool air does. The humidity of the air is also a contributory factor.

A mass of clay is composed of particles which lie near and upon each other with tunnels of air running through the mass. These tunnels, or 'capillaries' as they are called, are full of water when the clay is wet, and drying the clay consists of removing this water. Although a mass of unfired clay may be hard and appear dry it will still contain a good deal of water, particularly in the interior. It is not possible to remove all of the free water without raising the temperature of the clay. Drying is accompanied by shrinkage.

In the studio, forms are left to dry exposed to the air. If the form is dense or large it may be moved to a warm part of the room after a day or two. It is necessary to allow enough time for the water to be removed evenly throughout the clay. Should the form be placed so that one side becomes warmer than the other, near a kiln or in sunlight, then the form will distort as the warmer side becomes drier and consequently smaller. The same is true of a form which is placed where air is constantly moving past it, near a window or door, when the side against which the air flows will become dry. If these conditions cannot be avoided the form should be turned regularly to maintain balanced drying and shrinkage.

If clay is dried unevenly the form may crack apart owing to the considerable forces involved. If a thick form is dried too quickly the outer skin may shrink and crack as it becomes too small to cover the surface of the unshrunk interior. It is advisable to use coarse clay for large forms as the capillaries are larger and drying is easier.

The combined water releases only at temperatures above 350° C. But the exact temperature varies with each mineral present in the clay. It is generally accepted that most of the combined water is removed by the time the temperature reaches 550° C if the rise in temperature has been not more than 100° C per hour.

When the free water has been removed the clay form is very fragile and great care must be taken when handling it. Once the combined water is removed the clay will not return to a plastic state by the addition of free water. The combined water cannot be replaced.

The commonest fault in drying is warping, caused by uneven drying, and forms liable to warp should be turned regularly to allow even access of dry air to all surfaces. This refers particularly to tiles, slabs and thin cast or thrown forms.

Another common fault is cracking, caused by the junction of two clays either of unequal dryness or of different-sized capillaries, so that one dries more quickly than the other. Small cracks are modelled out by forcing the surrounding clay into the crack; larger ones can be filled with dry clay, similar to that of which the form is made. To fill very large cracks, use a mixture of dry clay, sand and grog with a little water to bind it together. Wet clay is unsuitable for filling cracks in dry forms as the filling clay will itself dry and shrink so producing more cracks.

BISQUIT PACKING AND FIRING

Once the clay has been dried it is placed in the kiln to be fired. The purpose of this firing is to harden the clay so that it may be easily glazed. Not all ceramics are bisquit-fired: the major exceptions are (high-fired) sanitary ware, salt-glazed ceramics and bricks. Normally the clay is fired to a temperature below that of the gloss. But it must reach its maturing temperature during one of these firings. An exception to this is bone china. As the bone-china body softens during firing, it is more economical to fire the ware to its highest temperature before spending time and money on decorating and glazing it.

With the exception of bone china, objects to be bisquited may touch each other in the kiln as there is no danger of the pieces sticking together. If the forms are strong enough they may be packed one inside the other or on top of each other. The forms will shrink as they dry and there is the chance that one piece may be locked inside another if there is not enough space between them.

Some kiln shelves and props may be used as necessary. Three props to a shelf will provide a strong and stable system.

Bisquit temperatures for each clay may vary and for satisfactory results it is necessary to pack only those clays which require the same firing. (The exact firing temperature

A bisquit kiln packed and ready for firing.

Several different types of kiln furniture, for stacking ware in the kiln. The five triangular stilts and the triangular bar (*bottom right*) are used to support glazed ware and prevent it from sticking to the shelves.

may be obtained from the supplier or determined by experiment.) As a rough guide, most soft bisquit is fired to between 1,000° and 1,140° C; red clays are usually the lower and white bodies the higher. In most studios a single compromise bisquit temperature – normally 1,050° C – is used as being most convenient.

Once the kiln has been packed with ware (this really amounts to simply placing the objects as economically as possible), remove the ventilating bung, in the top of the kiln, so that the kiln can be ventilated during the initial heating of the clay. The kiln can then be heated very gently (Simmerstat 20, three-way switch 'low' setting, gas kiln burners 20 per cent on) so that any water remaining in the clay may have time to evaporate. It therefore follows that the thicker the clay forms the slower should be the heating. For the same reason if the clay is of a very fine texture it should be subject to very slow initial heating. It is almost impossible to give definite times and temperature rises as these will vary from firing to firing. Nevertheless, as a guide, a bisquit kiln may be heated from room temperature to 500° C over a period of six hours. With thrown ware of slightly sanded clay the rise may be accelerated to occupy only five hours. In each case the rise is slower in the initial stages than in the later.

During this part of the bisquit firing the free water will be driven off. If the firing is too rapid the water will become superheated steam and generate such pressure that it will burst the clay form. This water will be driven off by the time the clay reaches the temperature of 300° C, but the chemically combined water will not be completely removed until the firing has reached 500° C. Until this latter temperature has been reached there will be a certain amount of steam generated inside the kiln and this will find its way out of the kiln even if the bung has not been removed. In the case of draught kilns other than muffle types this is not a problem. However, electric kilns are usually built inside a metal casing, which can become seriously corroded if the steam is permitted to escape only through the incidental cracks round the door. To keep this corrosion to a minimum the bung should always be removed in the initial stages of any firing, and replaced at about 500° C. Any water given off from clay, whether free or combined, will be acid in some degree and extremely corrosive.

Once the temperature has passed beyond 700° C the firing may be accelerated (e.g. Simmerstat 100, three-way switch 'high' setting, gas kiln burners on full) so as to maintain a rise of 100° C per hour, and this should continue until the kiln and the clay inside it have reached the desired temperature. The kiln may be allowed to soak for up to an hour at the top temperature but this is not always necessary.

Cooling

Normally a kiln will cool at a satisfactory rate if the fuel supply is cut off. The drop in temperature will probably be rapid in the early stages of cooling but this is in order for bisquit firing.

Once the temperature has dropped to 600° C the drop should be very slow and even until it is down to 500° C; again, the design of the kiln should accommodate this specification. Below 500° C the kiln should be allowed to cool at its own rate until it is down to 100° C, when the door may be eased open to introduce a slight draught and speed up the cooling, which is often very slow indeed at this stage.

Dunting or cracking can be caused by too rapid cooling of the bisquit especially between 600° and 500° C. This dunting may not be apparent until after the glaze has been applied and fired.

CHANGES IN CLAY DURING FIRING

The first change which occurs in clay when it is fired is the removal of the free water. This will be accompanied by the burning of any vegetable matter which is present in the form or the clay. It is followed by the removal of the combined water. The other changes are those which affect the minerals which make up the clay. All clays contain free silica in the form of sand, quartz or flint, and the crystals of silica are subject to changes in shape and volume at certain temperatures. Some of these changes are permanent (conversions), and others are reversible (inversions).

SILICA CHANGES ON HEATING

573° C Free silica form inverts to beta quartz and suddenly expands 1 per cent.

870° C Beta quartz starts to convert to beta cristobalite and beta tridymite, which occupy 16 per cent more volume than quartz.

SILICA CHANGES ON COOLING

870° C Conversion to cristobalite and tridymite ceases.

573° C Beta quartz inverts to alpha quartz and suddenly contracts 1 per cent.

220° C Beta cristobalite inverts to alpha cristobalite and suddenly contracts 3 per cent.

163° to 117° C Beta tridymite inverts to alpha tridymite and suddenly contracts 1 per cent.

The higher the clay is fired beyond 870° C the greater will be the proportion of cristobalite and tridymite in the cooled clay, so that most free silica will take the form of cristobalite and tridymite if it has been fired to 1,250° C or more, given sufficient time. This takes several weeks; most studio ceramic forms, when fired, contain about 10 per cent of the free silica as cristobalite and tridymite is rarely found. Once the clay has been fired the cristobalite and tridymite forms of silica will invert and expand at the same rate if reheated above their inversion points.

Minerals other than free silica will change, though less dramatically. Primarily these changes may be separated into those which take place below 800° C and those which occur above that temperature. The former reactions are primarily the release of gases as the clay minerals change and they need a well-ventilated kiln. The changes above 800° C occur as the alkalis in the clay act upon the silica and alumina to form a network of crystals (mullite) and glass which binds the undissolved material into a strong mass. This process is rarely completed in the soft bisquit firing.

When clay is fired to 1,300° C several changes occur. The most obvious one is that the body is harder when cooled and will probably be impervious to water: the clay is said to be 'vitrified'. This means that a high proportion of the material has melted and formed various combinations known as 'alumina-silicates'. The unmelted materials have crystalline forms and are suspended in the glass. One side-effect of this melting is that all the spaces between the un-dissolved particles become filled and there is a resultant shrinkage of the over-all size of the clay form. The higher the clay is fired the greater the shrinkage and the lower the porosity. Also, the higher the clay is fired the greater will be its contraction and expansion during subsequent cooling or reheating, as the free silica changes shape and volume.

A clay which does not vitrify without considerable heat (say 1,300° C) is said to be 'refractory'. Fire clays are refractory, and clays which may be fired to stoneware temperatures are more refractory than those which may only be fired to earthenware temperatures. Any clay can be melted if subjected to sufficient heat. The ideal is to fire each type of clay to the point of maximum vitrification without deformation. In practice, vitrification cannot be completed without distortion and the reactions of the melting minerals are arrested at a point where maximum strength has been achieved without loss of form.

There are two types of fault in bisquit firing.

Firing too rapidly. The clay forms will have blown apart with cracks producing slivers of clay across the surface of the form as if a small explosion has taken place within the wall of the form. This is caused by not allowing sufficient time for the free water to evaporate.

Cooling too rapidly. As will be seen from the notes on silica inversions, there are several points where the clay form undergoes sudden changes in volume. If the form is hotter on one surface than another it may crack when one half changes volume and the other does not. Time must be allowed for these changes to occur as slowly and evenly as possible to avoid splitting the ware. This fault should be rare if the kiln is not unpacked before the temperature within it has dropped to 100° C.

Blown ware – the result of firing a bisquit kiln with the simmerstat accidentally left on '100'.

English Liverpool porcelain bowl. Slip-cast, painted with cobalt oxide on white clay under a transparent porcelain glaze.

English Staffordshire creamer, eighteenth century. Slip-cast, coloured with oxides applied with a sponge.

13 Changing the surface after bisquit firing

There are many reasons why the decorative processes which can be put to use before firing the clay for the first time are not sufficient in themselves. The commonest reason, in the pottery industry, is that it would be wasteful to spend time and energy in decorating ware which might crack, dunt or deform during the first firing. For the studio ceramist any previously untried form may have faults in the design or manufacturing process which reveal themselves only after firing. Similarly, any new material or combination of materials may reveal unexpected characteristics after being bisquited. The economic need to keep the kiln fully loaded may mean that some of the objects have to be fired before there is time to decorate them. Sometimes the forms which are made are in themselves so fragile that it is essential to fire them before they can be handled without the risk of damage. This is certainly the case where the objects are to be handled by unskilled persons, unfamiliar with the fragile nature of dry, unfired clay.

With the exception of bone china the bisquited ware should still be porous enough to absorb water, which is essential if the glaze is to be easily applied. The porous surface is easy to paint with oxides to produce areas of colour, but as the brushmarks tend to appear in the fired surface, the painting must be done with great care to avoid unwanted marks or textures. As with painting on unfired clay, the quality of the brushes is most important if good-quality results are desired.

Oxides or manufactured colours tend to become mixed with the glaze when this is applied. If the glaze is applied by dipping the form into a tub of glaze solution, there is a danger that some of the colour will come away from the form and contaminate the batch of glaze. For this reason it is usual to use a gum (usually gum arabic dissolved in water) as the painting medium so that the colour is firmly attached to the form. Oxide painted without a gum medium is very easily damaged by careless handling. A side-effect of this is that the painted area is no longer porous, and care must be taken in the glazing process to ensure an even and dense covering of glaze over the painted areas. It may be necessary to refire painted bisquit to 850° C, to drive off the gum and harden the oxide onto the clay.

Apart from direct painting, colour may be applied by using a spray gun with an extractor unit to produce bands of

Late seventeenth-century teapot by
Elers. Moulded form with applied
design, high fired but unglazed.

colour which may be faded out and appear as patches, or
rainbow effects of one colour fading into another. The spray
technique can be used in conjunction with paper stencils or
any other perforated surface.

Once an area of colour has been applied it may be worked
into by scratching the surface with a sharp-pointed stick.
The marks made are much weaker than those similarly made
on unfired clay.

ENGOBES

Engobes may be applied to bisquited ware provided that the
composition is suitable; a formula for an engobe which can
be applied to bisquit will be found on page 106. If the engobe
is applied by dipping (see page 107) or pouring (see page 154),
its thickness will depend on the porosity of the bisquit and
the viscosity of the engobe solution.

An engobe can also be sprayed onto the bisquit clay. In this case it may be quite liquid as it can be built up in layers and, if necessary, dried between each layer. Again stencils may be used and provided they do not touch the surface of the clay several colours can be applied without the necessity of firing the form after each application. An unfired engobe has a very weak bond with a bisquit clay, and if the stencil touches the sprayed but unfired engobe surface there is a real danger that the fragile coating will be marked or broken so that it falls away, revealing a bare patch of clay. Once this has happened it is very difficult to repair.

With the spray gun several types of textured surface are possible. If the gun is held about two feet away from the surface which is being sprayed, a fine mist should be deposited onto the form, as the larger particles lose momentum across this distance and fall down before they reach the target.

If the gun is held closer to a spinning clay form, a fluffy texture will build up, composed of separate particles, some of which can be quite large.

GRINDING

It may be necessary to fettle the form by grinding, if it is too fragile in the green or dry state. This may also be necessary with geometric forms which cannot be accurately shaped in the unfired state. The process of grinding is common in the electrical porcelain industry, where accuracy in dimension and shape is vital.

There are several different methods of grinding ceramics, from the simple alumina block – commonly available to the studio ceramist – to diamond cutting wheels. If necessary, a potter's wheel can be converted to a grinding or lapidary's wheel by fixing a carborundum disc to the wheelhead. It is essential in all cutting and grinding of ceramics to see that the cutting agent does not mark or discolour the clay surface. Soft-fired clay may be rubbed with sandpaper to remove any rough edges.

14 Glazes

Ceramics has been described as the art of arrested reactions, and nowhere is this more apparent than in the case of glazes.

A glaze is a form of glass so constituted that, when applied to a clay form and heated sufficiently, it will melt without melting the clay, and when cooled will have a thermal expansion similar to that of the clay. In fact this is relatively easy as the ingredients for the glass are those elements which are also present in different proportions in the clay itself. The higher the temperature at which the glazing reaction takes place the greater the similarity between the clay and the glaze.

We have seen (page 24) that clay is largely composed of alumina and silica in various forms. In a glaze the silica is the glass-making material and the alumina and other ingredients act upon the silica to produce a glaze. Obviously

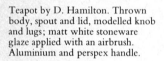

Teapot by D. Hamilton. Thrown body, spout and lid, modelled knob and lugs; matt white stoneware glaze applied with an airbrush. Aluminium and perspex handle.

Bowl by S. Hamada, 1927. Diameter 20 cm. Thrown, with an engraved image, glazed with a light celadon crackle glaze.

Bottle by S. Hamada, 1927. Height 26 cm. Thrown, glazed with a stoneware iron-black glaze with iron oxide painted over.

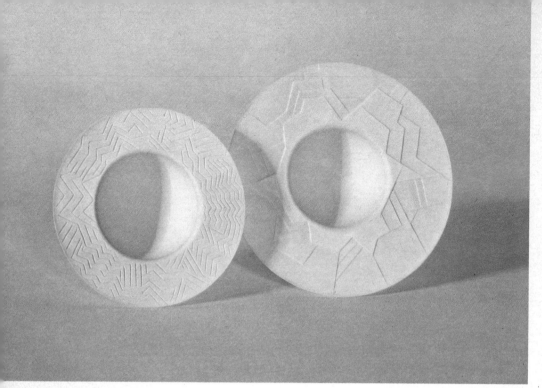

Two bowls by J. Poncelet. Slip-cast in layers
of blue and white slip with
sgraffito image, unglazed.

Shepherds' Dance bowl by T. S. Haile, 1937.
Diameter 32 cm. Thrown in coarse
clay, painted with oxides under a
stoneware light celadon glaze.

if the temperature at which this reaction is satisfactorily completed is too high the clay form will lose its shape. Therefore there must be a third element which will promote a similar reaction but within an acceptable temperature range. There are several different substances which will act in this way, and they are called 'fluxes'. It is also known that if more than one flux is used, a phenomenon called 'eutectic' will further lower the temperature at which the materials will fuse (or reduce the amount of flux necessary to produce a melt at the same temperature).

EUTECTIC

MATERIAL/MIXTURE		MELTING–POINT
lead oxide	alone	876° C
silica	alone	1,710° C
boric oxide	alone	294° C
lead oxide	94%	526° C
silica	6%	
lead oxide	60%	661° C
silica	40%	
lead oxide	88%	493° C
boric oxide	12%	
lead oxide	61%	768° C
boric oxide	39%	

When applied to a clay form the glaze is in a powder state. The powder is suspended in water to facilitate the application of the glaze to the clay form, but the water will not play a part in the fusibility of the glaze materials unless it is heavily loaded with soluble minerals. The glaze goes through several identifiable phases before it finally forms a liquid coating over the clay:

(a) The glaze will dry to a state of dehydration above 500° C.

(b) Any carbonates or sulphides combined with the glaze-forming materials will give off gases at various stages of the heating.

(c) The materials will sinter and harden so that they are bonded together, and to the clay, several hundred degrees before the final melting temperature.

(d) The sintered material will gradually soften 200° or 300° C below the finishing temperature.

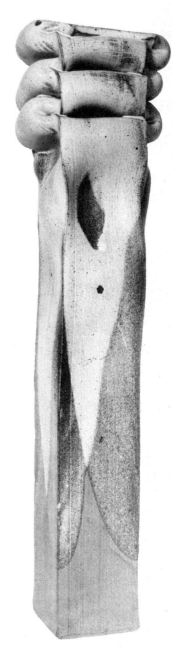

Extruded and folded column, by D. Hamilton. Iron-bearing body with slabbed base, glazed by pouring matt white glaze to produce overlapping areas. The iron from the body burns through the glaze where it is thin.

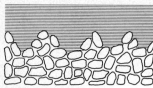

Earthenware

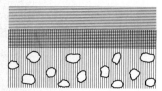

Stoneware

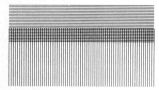

Porcelain

Clay-glaze interface.

(*e*) The melting materials will boil, in varying degrees according to the ingredients, before they melt to a liquid.

At the same time the clay which constitutes the form of the object undergoes changes (see page 117).

When the heating of the glaze has ceased the liquid starts to harden, but this is a gradual change. In a liquid state the glaze fits the clay, i.e. it covers the glaze surface. As the glaze and clay continue to cool the glaze will harden and both clay and glaze will shrink. Even when apparently quite hard a glaze will stretch or compress within limits as it tries to hold on to the clay. If the thermal expansion of the glaze and clay are too dissimilar then glaze faults will occur (see page 138).

The glaze holds to the clay by means of its physical grip on the clay form but, more importantly, by seeping into the surface of the clay and filling some of the open pores. When a section of an earthenware form is examined it will be seen that a distinct line separates the glaze and clay. In a stoneware form the line of separation is indistinct and in true porcelain the fusion of the glaze and clay is so complete that there is little or no demarcation between the two. The development of this interface is important in promoting the smooth covering of the clay by the glaze and in its remaining on the form. Poor development of the clay/glaze interface may lead to glaze faults, particularly crawling (see page 140).

All the above reactions require time as well as heat for their full development. The only method of measuring this relationship between time and temperature is by the use of pyrometric cones (see page 41), but most glazes have such a wide range of firing temperature that other measuring devices can give satisfactory results.

From this description it is evident that there are a great many reactions which take place during the firing of glaze, and the nature of the kiln firing, too, may bring about variations (see Chapter 17).

GLAZE INGREDIENTS

It would be possible to mix up a glaze using refined and pure chemicals but apart from the expense involved, the resulting glaze would not necessarily develop the desired characteristics. There are many minerals which contain one or more glaze-making elements and these, rather than pure elements, normally figure in glaze recipes.

The recipes on page 178 may be used as a basis for experiments in changing the glaze surface and colour. (Colouring of glazes is dealt with in the next chapter.) It should be remembered that for thousands of years ceramists produced glaze surfaces of great beauty without the advantage of chemical analysis. Experiments along the lines indicated by descriptions of the action of the various minerals should produce a wide variety of glazes.

As we have seen, most glazes consist of fluxes, alumina and silica. As a general rule it should be remembered that the greater the amount of alumina, and silica in particular, the higher will be the firing temperature of the glaze. While the alumina and silica come from clay minerals and flint, fluxes are available from a great variety of mineral sources.

Fluxes

The following compounds are active fluxes in glazes when fired within the temperatures indicated. If a high-temperature flux is added to a low-temperature glaze it will not be very active, and if present in sufficient quantities may produce a glaze with an underfired or matt appearance.

| | TEMPERATURE/ RANGE (° C) | | | | THERMAL |
	MIN.	MAX.	TOXIC	SOLUBLE	EXPANSION
lead oxide	800	1,180	yes	slightly	low
potassium oxide	900	1,400	no	yes	high
sodium oxide	850	1,400	no	yes	high
boric oxide	800	1,400	no	yes	very low
zinc oxide	1,050	1,400	yes	no	low
calcium oxide	1,100	1,400	no	no	medium
barium oxide	1,150	1,400	yes	no	medium
magnesium oxide	1,150	1,400	no	no	very low

The choice of flux for a glaze at a given temperature will depend on the type of colour and surface desired in the glaze as well as the temperature to which the glaze is to be fired.

Most glazes depending on fluxes with a high thermal expansion will craze (see page 133) over most clays but give colours unobtainable with other fluxes.

Frits

Some materials are commonly available in fritted form if the main constituent is naturally soluble. Soluble materials are difficult to handle when mixed with other glaze ingredients and water as they tend to crystallize out of the solution, which results in an uneven application of the ingredients to the form. The frit usually combines the required element and silica (as this is necessary in all glazes) and is made by melting the ingredients in a furnace. When cooled and ground to a fine powder the material produced is insoluble and non-toxic.

Frits are common in low-temperature glazes (up to 1,140° C) but beyond this temperature minerals are used where possible. Many are available which combine fluxes with silica as natural frits. Common frits necessitated by the soluble nature of the desired element are alkaline, containing potassium, sodium and borax. Lead is used in fritted form as in its raw state it is toxic and dangerous to use in the studio. Low-solubility lead frits contain borax and lead.

Occurrence and effect of various fluxing elements:

Barium, toxic: A secondary flux in low-temperature glazes. A slight flux in high-temperature glazes. Used to produce matt or dry glazes but will not do so in the presence of boric oxide. *Colour:* helps in the development of copper-blue glazes.

Boron: An active flux at all temperatures. Used in fritted form as it is soluble. Normally produces glazes with good craze resistance. In combination with lead, borax gives a hard-wearing, trouble-free, commercial-type glaze for use at low temperatures. *Colour:* it intensifies colour but may produce mottling. With iron it may produce opalescent glazes. Favours the development of turquoise from copper.

Calcium: A secondary flux in low-temperature glazes. Main flux in high-temperature glazes but not usually used alone. It makes the resulting glaze hard-wearing. *Colour:* helps in developing the colour of celadon glazes.

Lead, toxic: A low-temperature flux which starts to vaporize at 1,170° C. It produces trouble-free glazes with good craze resistance. It must be fired in an oxidizing or neutral atmosphere. Gives a lustrous glaze surface. Normally used in fritted form because of health hazards. In a raw state it is easily absorbed into the bloodstream and some lead glazes give up small but dangerous amounts of lead into acid food and drink. *Colour:* it allows a wide variety of colours, but glazes for tableware must not be coloured with copper as this greatly increases the solubility of the lead in the glaze.

Magnesium: A high-temperature flux but best with at least one other flux. In excess it may produce crawl in glazes. *Colour:* Tends to produce purple or red from cobalt at very high temperatures.

Potassium: A strong alkaline flux at all temperatures; similar to sodium in many respects, and often blended with it in alkaline frits. Produces soft glazes with a tendency to craze. *Colour:* similar to sodium but favours blue/purple from manganese.

Sodium: A strong flux at all temperatures. Used in fritted form as it is soluble. Produces glazes which tend to craze and which are not hard-wearing. *Colour:* promotes brilliant colour and favours turquoise from copper and red/purple from manganese.

Zinc, toxic: Used to produce crypto-crystalline matt glazes at low temperatures (see page 148). A flux when used in small quantities in high-temperature glazes as it helps the other ingredients to melt. An important ingredient in crystal glazes. In excess, zinc will make glazes crawl and pinhole (see page 140). *Colour:* copper produces turquoise in zinc glazes. Chrome will produce brown in the presence of zinc.

Materials commonly used to contribute the necessary elements in glaze recipes:

Alkaline frit: A blend of sodium, potassium and silica which renders the sodium and potassium insoluble. It makes the elements easier to mix with other glaze ingredients. Most alkaline glazes will craze, so various proportions of borax may be included in the frit to decrease the thermal expansion of the finished glaze. Follow the manufacturer's instructions for satisfactory results. *Colour:* favours turquoise from copper and purple from manganese.

Ash: Thoroughly burnt vegetable matter. Varies in composition according to the type of plant but major elements are silica, alumina and alkaline fluxes with small proportions of metallic oxides. Some types will produce a glaze at 1,250° C without further additions.

Alumina hydrate: A form of pure alumina. Used as a bat wash to prevent glaze from adhering to kiln shelves, and very rarely to add alumina to glaze.

Ball clay: Added to bodies to increase plasticity and may be used to introduce alumina and silica into glazes, particularly raw glazes, as it helps to suspend the glaze material in the water of solution.

Barium carbonate, toxic: A secondary flux in high-temperature glazes, up to 10 per cent. Produces mattness if present at 10–20 per cent and in the absence of boric oxide. Alkaline response to colouring oxides.

Bentonite: A very plastic ball clay used as a suspension agent in glazes, 2–3 per cent.

Borax frit: An artificial material compounded to make boric oxide convenient to use. Includes silica and a little alkaline flux. Follow the manufacturer's instructions for normal results.

Calcium borate (colmanite or borocalcite): A natural frit of boric and calcium oxides. A powerful low-temperature flux at 5–40 per cent and a secondary high-temperature flux at 5–15 per cent.

Calcium carbonate (chalk, whiting): A flux in high-temperature glazes at up to 25 per cent, but more than 35 per cent will start to matt the glaze.

Calcium magnesium carbonate (dolomite): A secondary flux in high-temperature glaze at 5–25 per cent.

Calcium phosphate (bone ash): A secondary flux in high-temperature glazes at 5–10 per cent. An important ingredient in bone-china bodies.

China clay (kaolin): A white firing form of non-plastic clay.

An important ingredient in clay bodies, used to introduce alumina and silica into glaze at 5–25 per cent.

China stone (Cornish stone): Similar to felspar but contains more silica. A high-temperature flux and a secondary flux at low temperatures. Several types are available.

Felspar: An insoluble mineral containing sodium, potassium, alumina and silica; there are several types. A secondary flux at low temperatures, 10–40 per cent, and a primary flux at high temperatures. About 50 per cent felspar content is usual in stoneware glazes, but there may be as much as 80 per cent. Some types may produce a glaze at 1,250° C without further additions.

Flint: A form of pure silica. Some of the silica necessary for a satisfactory glaze will be provided by other glaze ingredients but it may be 'topped up' with up to 15 per cent flint at low temperatures and 30 per cent at high.

Lead bisilicate, toxic: A combination of lead and silica in a fritted form in order to reduce the hazard to the user from lead poisoning. Usually the proportions in the bisilicate are lead 65 per cent, silica 35 per cent. It may be present in low-temperature glazes (about 1,080° C) up to 90 per cent. Colour: favours apple-green from copper and brown and tan from iron.

Lead frit: An active flux, which usually includes borax and flint, at low temperatures giving satisfactory glazes if not fired in a reducing atmosphere or above 1,180° C. Should not be coloured with copper oxide for use on tableware. Follow the supplier's instructions for satisfactory results.

Magnesium carbonate: A high-temperature flux. Up to 10 per cent may be added to produce a smooth, buttery surface to the glaze but more than this will produce mattness.

Magnesium silicate: A secondary flux at all temperatures but it may produce mattness if it is present in large quantities.

Nepheline syenite: A very fusible felspar. 10 per cent of nepheline syenite has the same melting properties as 15 per cent of normal felspar.

Quartz: Another form of pure silica, which may often be used in the place of flint. 5–20 per cent in low-temperature glazes, 15–30 per cent in high-temperature glazes.

Sodium carbonate (soda ash): A soluble form of sodium, rarely used except in a fritted form.

Sodium chloride (common salt): A form of sodium used in salt glazing.

Volcanic ash: A fusible rock of varying composition which has been melted at the time of its deposition. Used in high-temperature glazes at 10 per cent for a smooth, opaque surface, 50 per cent for a fluid, clear glaze.

Zinc oxide: Used in small amounts, up to 5 per cent in high-temperature glazes to assist in the melt and in all glazes to produce mattness, 5–15 per cent in non-boracic glazes.

A glaze is classified according to its major characteristics, namely

> the temperature to which it is fired,
> the texture of the glazed surface,
> the colour of the fired glaze,
> the major flux.

Temperature. Glazes fired no higher than 1,150° C are classified as 'earthenware' glazes. Those fired above 1,150° C are called 'stoneware' or 'porcelain' glazes.

Texture. Glazes may be shiny (or glossy), matt or semi-matt (see page 148).

Colour. The colour may range from bright red to muted browns and blacks. It may also be textured or a combination of several different colours. The colour may depend on the type of flux which is used to produce the glass content of the glaze. Alkaline fluxes will produce certain characteristic colours when the colouring oxides are added (see Chapter 15).

Major flux. Glazes may be further classified by the major active constituent, e.g. lead, ash, boracic and slip glazes.

When the body from which the form is made has certain outstanding characteristics these may also be identified. For instance, 'bone china' identifies the clay body, but a bone-china glaze is an earthenware glaze which is compatible with the bone-china body. A porcelain glaze may be an ordinary stoneware glaze which will withstand the temperature to which porcelain body is fired.

EARTHENWARE GLAZES

Some of the earliest known earthenware glazes seem to have occurred where the material used to form the object included sufficient alkaline material to produce a thin skin of glaze on the fired surface. There is also evidence of fritted alkaline glazes in the Near East *c.* 2000 BC. Lead in the form of galena (a lead ore containing iron as an impurity) was common in the Middle Ages in Europe. Sodium and potassium are the commonest fluxes, together with lead and boron.

Alkaline glazes

The most convenient form of alkaline glaze is one based on a commercial frit, of which many different types are available. It is necessary to ensure that the frit or glaze purchased will produce a glaze at the desired temperature. Most alkaline glazes will craze over most clays and are not suitable for low-fired tableware. Some commercial glazes are 'craze-resistant' but the degree of crazing will depend on the care taken during the bisquit and gloss firings (see page 139).

Lead glazes

Lead has been the most popular earthenware flux as it produces a smooth, deep satin gloss and has a thermal expansion very similar to that of clay. The introduction of fritted glazes has reduced the danger, for the ceramist, of contracting lead poisoning, but the solubility of lead in low-fired glazes is now revealed as a potential hazard for any one eating or drinking acid solutions from a lead-glazed surface. Nevertheless, if the glaze is well fired and copper is not used to colour it, it should remain safe. Otherwise it should be used only on non-functional forms, and this is certainly the case with low-fired glazes made from unfritted lead, e.g. raku (see page 170).

Boracic glazes

These glazes are glossy and do not have the same tendency to craze that alkaline glazes have. Borax boils considerably before melting and may give a mottled surface when coloured with metal oxides. The colours produced in boracic glazes are usually alkaline. Follow the supplier's instructions for satisfactory use.

STONEWARE GLAZES

High-fired glazes originated in China and it is likely that, with wood as the fuel for the fire, some of the wood ash would carry on to the clay forms and melt some of the free silica in the body, thus forming a glaze.

The use of felspar as a fluxing and glaze-making material also originated in the Far East. As the stoneware forms were fired in open-fired kilns using solid fuel, the atmosphere of the kiln was normally starved of oxygen, thus producing a 'reduction atmosphere' which affected the surface of the glaze and the colour produced by metallic oxides where they were present. Reduction stoneware glazes are still favoured by ceramists. Some glazes produce satisfactory results only in certain atmospheric conditions and these conditions must be induced in modern kilns which burn fuel efficiently.

ASH GLAZES

Wood ash will vary in composition but the first test should be to determine whether it will produce a glaze without any additions. To do this, clean the ash by soaking it in an excess of water for twenty-four hours, after which any foreign matter may be removed. The ash should then be dried and crushed. The soaking (or washing) may be repeated if necessary, but if the ash is washed more than

(*Opposite*) Chinese ewer, Sung Dynasty. Thrown and modelled form with sgraffito design under a transparent glaze.

twice, too much of the soluble flux may be washed away. Pass the ash and water solution through a 200-mesh sieve before use. Some of this solution may be fired in an unglazed bowl, to avoid spoiling other forms in the kiln if the glass should be too liquid when fired to 1,250° C. Normally felspar is used with wood ash to produce a good glaze.

According to the fluidity and thickness of the glaze produced by ash alone, it is possible to reduce the proportion of ash to as little as 40 per cent, adding up to 50 per cent of felspar, up to 15 per cent of china clay or up to 15 per cent of flint.

FELSPATHIC GLAZES

Stoneware felspathic glazes vary in composition but the main ingredients include felspar, china clay, whiting and flint or quartz. The proportions vary between 55 per cent of felspar and other fluxes to 45 per cent flint or quartz and clay – which gives a dry glaze – and 85 per cent to 15 per cent respectively, for glossy glazes. If the ratio of flint to clay is high, the glaze will be shiny and hard; if low, it will have a matt texture.

Most felspathic glazes include some whiting (5–20 per cent) and some or all of this may be replaced by one or more of the following secondary fluxes:

barium carbonate	5%	to 10%
colemanite	5%	to 10%
dolomite	5%	to 15%
zinc oxide	1%	to 6%
magnesium carbonate	2%	to 7%
talc	5%	to 15%

The greater the number of fluxes the more active they will be.

SLIP GLAZES

Some clays, particularly those which mature at very low temperatures, may be suitable for conversion to slip glazes for stoneware firing. Iron-bearing (red) clays are commonly used for this purpose; after trying the clay fired on its own, felspar may be added, up to 50 per cent. Not all clays will give good results, and only those which melt to a great extent without any addition would be worth pursuing. Other suitable fluxes may be added, which may alter the colour of the glaze. Slip glazes are ideal for application to unfired clay, as they have similar shrinkage from wet to dry, and so the forms can be brought to their finished state in one firing.

Scales for weighing large quantities of ceramic materials (*rear*) and balances for small amounts (*front*).

Various sieves and lawn brushes.

GLAZE PREPARATION

To prepare the glaze, weigh out the ingredients carefully, on balances for small quantities or on scales for large amounts. Put the ingredients into a bowl or plastic bucket and cover them with enough water to produce a creamy solution. Excess water, added accidentally, can be siphoned off or removed with a sponge, if the solution is allowed to settle overnight. If left overnight the ingredients will slake down to a smooth paste. The solution of material and water should then be sieved into a clean bowl through a 150-mesh or 200-mesh sieve to break up any lumps and to ensure an even dispersion of the various materials in the glaze solution. If it is difficult to get the material through the sieve, brush it through by stirring the glaze in the sieve with a stiff brush. If there are any hard lumps which will not pass

137

Hand grinding tools for glaze and colouring materials: mortars and pestles (*rear*); palette knives and glazed tile (*bottom left*); mullers and a glass slab (*bottom right*).

A ball mill and jars and grinding media. Any material, particularly glazes which include colouring oxides, may be ground to a fine particle size by placing it in the jar with the media and allowing it to rotate for several hours.

through, these may be removed and ground in a mortar with a pestle or ball-milled, though too much ball-milling can contribute to the glaze fault known as 'crawling' (see page 140). When the solution has passed twice through the sieve the glaze is ready for use. To produce consistent results, it is essential that none of the material weighed out be accidentally discarded.

GLAZE FAULTS

There are several types of glaze fault which may become evident either immediately after firing or some time afterwards. In the case of crazing it may take months or years for the fault to appear. Delayed crazing in earthenware is commonly attributed to the absorption of atmospheric water by the clay, which causes it to expand and crack the glaze. Other faults in fired ware may be attributable to a fault in the manufacturing, application, or firing process rather than in the formulation of the glaze.

Crazing. The commonest fault in glazed surfaces is termed 'crazing' from the network of cracks which develop in the cooled glaze surface. It most often occurs in earthenware alkaline glazes but may also be found in stoneware glazes. The greater the frequency of the cracks the greater is the problem. The fault is caused by the glaze having a greater thermal expansion and contraction than the body, so that it becomes too small to cover the clay on cooling.

To avoid crazing the thermal expansion of the clay should be slightly greater than that of the glaze. The thermal expansion of the glaze is determined by that of the fluxing agents, and the proportion of flint, in the glaze. That of the body is determined by the amount of free silica and the crystalline form which it takes. The heat work to which the clay is subjected during the glaze or the bisquit firing will determine the proportion of each type of silica crystal present at the end of the glaze firing (see page 118).

To increase the thermal expansion of the body more free silica in the form of flint must be added to it, and wedged or pugged into the body. In the studio this is an inconvenient process: apart from the labour involved, most clay bodies are used for several glazes and to change the thermal expansion of the clay for one glaze may result in glaze faults when

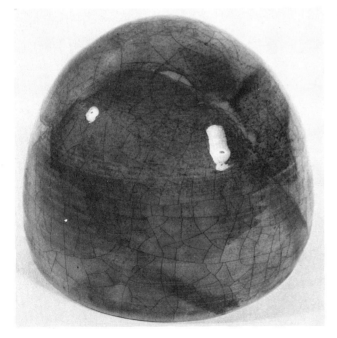

An example of crazed glaze.

using other glazes which have previously been satisfactory. An alternative solution is to fire the bisquit higher or soak it at the top temperature, which will allow more silica to change type. This may. however, create difficulties when the glaze is to be applied, as the porosity of the body may be decreased (see page 118).

To change the thermal expansion of the glaze more silica may be added. This does not behave like free silica in the body but is melted by the fluxes and forms various silicates in the glaze, lowering its thermal expansion. By adding more silica to the glaze the melting-point may be raised, but this may be disadvantageous in low-fired glazes. The only alternative is to change some or all of the flux for one which has a lower thermal expansion (see page 129). If this means that the final colour of the fired glaze is not that which is wanted, then the crazing will have to be accepted as un-avoidable.

Peeling is the exact opposite of crazing but is much rarer. It too is identified by a network of cracks all over the fired glaze surface but when a hand is rubbed across them the cracks can be felt to be raised above the glaze. This is caused by the body having a much greater thermal expansion than the glaze. It shrinks on cooling so that the glaze cracks in attempting to remain on the clay and compressive forces cause the separate plates of glaze to overlap. In severe cases the glaze may become detached from the clay body.

To prevent peeling, either decrease the amount of free silica in the body, which is impossible in the studio unless clay bodies are made up rather than bought ready for use, or decrease the firing temperature of the bisquit or glaze firing.

Alternatively the thermal expansion of the glaze may be increased by changing all or some of the flux for one which has a higher thermal expansion (see page 129).

Crawling can be diagnosed if the glaze, when fired, gathers up into nodules to reveal unglazed areas. It is caused by poor adhesion between the body and the glaze during the melting. If the glaze is naturally viscous with a high surface tension – e.g. glazes high in zinc or tin or ground too finely – the only cure is to apply the glaze very thinly. Other causes are dust on the bisquit which prevents the glaze from attaching itself to the clay when applied (a common cause) or traces of oil or grease on the bisquit due to careless handling between bisquit firing and application of the glaze. To avoid this, ensure that the bisquit is glazed as soon as possible after being fired and that your hands are clean when handling it.

Damp bisquit may also cause poor glaze adhesion so it is advisable to allow the bisquit to dry after the first surface, inner or outer, has been glazed. If the glaze contains a lot of natural clay in the recipe this may cause the unfired glaze to shrink excessively during the drying stages, and small cracks will appear in it. If this happens, change some or all

Plaster spit-out which appeared two months after the piece was finished.

An example of crawled glaze.

of the clay for a calcined type or one which has a very small shrinkage from wet to dry: for example, exchange ball clay for china clay or china clay for calcined china clay. Zinc glazes may also shrink excessively when drying. Any cracks which do appear in unfired glaze should be smoothed and filled by rubbing with a clean finger.

Dunting, which is cracking of the fired form during or after cooling, may be caused by glazes with different thermal expansions being applied to the outer and inner surfaces of the form. If a matt glaze (particularly the zinc matt type) is applied to a thin clay form the compressive forces in the finished glaze may be strong enough to split the form. Dunting is also caused by thermal shock (see page 119).

Pinholing is identified by small or large holes in the surface of the glaze, caused by the boiling which all glazes undergo during melting. Some fluxes will boil more than others: lithium, for instance, is a flux not much used in studios for this reason. Sometimes the pinholes are so small that they fog the glaze and pinholing can be identified only upon close examination.

The cure for pinholing is to soak the kiln, when the glaze has reached its top temperature, so that the glaze has time to boil and settle. Alternatively the flux in the glaze may be changed for another which boils less.

Bubbling of the glaze, so that it comes from the gloss kiln with a surface like the skin of a toad, is caused by the same reaction as that which causes pinholing and the cure is the same.

Plaster spit-out is not really a glaze fault, but is revealed sometimes after the final firing. It takes the form of a crater appearing in an otherwise satisfactory surface. A white lump will be found lying inside the crater; this is plaster of paris which has found its way into the clay during the preparation or forming process. When the plaster is fired it

Chinese Kuan ware bowl, Sung Dynasty. Thrown form with deliberately crazed (crackle) glaze.

becomes dehydrated but on cooling will absorb atmospheric moisture very easily. Consequently it will expand and the increase in volume creates a pressure sufficient to 'spit-out' a piece of the surface. There is no cure – only prevention.

Other glaze faults are normally attributable to poor glaze application (too thick or too thin) or underfiring or overfiring the glaze so that it is either dry like sandpaper or runs off the surface of the clay and forms pools at the base.

All glaze reactions commonly identified as faults may nevertheless be used for their surface quality, particularly when overlaid with another glaze and refired.

15 Colour and texture in glazes

Colour in ceramics is achieved by the presence of oxides or salts of metal. Sometimes these metals, particularly iron, are present in the clay in some form. When this is the case the glaze applied over the clay may be influenced by the body. When a transparent glaze is applied over a dark firing clay (such as red earthenware clay) the glaze colour will be a shade of brown or black. Even if the glaze is coloured the final colour will be very dark unless a white opacifier is added to the glaze.

The colour of unfired metal oxides will bear little or no relation to the colour produced in the glaze. This may be easier to grasp if it is remembered that colour is determined by the light waves which are reflected and refracted by the surface of the form. Metal oxides modify the characteristics of the glaze surface.

There are many commercial preparations available to the modern ceramist, sold under the names of 'glaze stains', 'underglaze colours' and 'on-glaze colours'. They are compounds of metal oxides, fluxes and refractory material which when used according to the manufacturers' instructions will produce the specified colour. While these are satisfactory for many purposes, they do not have the flexibility of use which is possible with metal oxides.

All metallic oxides can be used to colour clays, engobes and glazes, or they may be applied over or under a glaze. Obviously it is pointless to apply a colouring oxide over a dark-firing clay with the intention of producing an image which is clear and precise. If this is desired, a white engobe or glaze should be first applied over the clay to give a surface suitable for the application of such colour.

Various hues and tones of colour are made possible by the addition of several colouring oxides to a single engobe or glaze, and interesting combinations of one coloured glaze with another can be found by experiment. The type of firing to which coloured glazes are subjected may play an important part in determining the type of colour which is produced. Some oxides are stable at all firing temperatures but others may tend to volatilize at high temperatures. Certain oxides will produce widely different colours in glazes according to the amount of oxygen present in the atmosphere in which they are fired. Finally, the major flux in the glaze may determine the particular type of colour produced.

Broken colour can be produced by the addition to the glaze of texturing material such as rutile or ilmenite. Different types of colour break-up can occur naturally when a coloured glaze is applied unevenly, particularly when it is applied over a dark-burning clay. When one glaze is applied over another the colour of the underglaze may break through the upper glaze, producing a variegated surface. Matt glazes (see page 148) are particularly prone to do this when applied over a more liquid glaze. Glazes which rely on borax as the flux may produce a mottled surface when coloured because of the intense boiling which precedes the melting.

The following is a list of colours and the metal oxides which may be used to achieve them:

Red	Cadmium and selenium fired below 1,050° C
	Copper oxide when fired in a reduction firing
	Potassium bichromate fired below 950° C
	Iron
	Uranium
Pink	Combinations of chrome and tin
	Combinations of gold chloride and tin chloride fired below 1,100° C
Orange	Combinations of cadmium and selenium
	Potassium bichromate
	Uranium
Yellow	Combinations of cadmium and selenium
	Iron
	Vanadium pentoxide with tin
	Antimony oxide
	Uranium
Green	Copper
	Chrome
	Iron in small quantities in a stoneware reduction firing (see page 163)
Turquoise	Copper in alkaline glazes
	Copper and cobalt in alkaline glazes
Blue	Cobalt
	Copper
	Cobalt with nickel
	Iron
Purple	Manganese in alkaline glazes
	Manganese with cobalt
Brown	Iron
	Manganese in lead glazes
	Chrome in zinc glazes
	Nickel
White	Tin
	Zirconium
Cream	Titanium
Black	Combination of any three of cobalt, iron, manganese, copper, to a total not exceeding 8 to 10 per cent
	Iron in stoneware glazes, 10 per cent

(*Opposite*) *Triumphant Procession* by T. S. Haile, 1937. Height 41 cm. A thrown jar in a coarse clay, painted with oxides under a transparent stoneware glaze.

Some of these colours are elusive and will depend upon the type of flux, either primary or secondary, in the glaze, and on firing to the correct temperature and in a suitable atmosphere. Each of the several possibilities will produce a different type of the desired colour.

Metal oxides differ in their colouring ability. The indicated percentages in the following list should be regarded as normal upper and lower limits.

Antimoniate of lead, toxic: 5–10 per cent will produce yellow in lead glazes.

Antimony oxide, toxic: 7–17 per cent will produce white. In lead glazes it tends to produce yellow as some antimoniate of lead is formed.

Cadmium, toxic: Cadmium is normally combined with selenium to produce red, orange or yellow glazes. Because of the difficulty of handling the material it is best to purchase a glaze or glaze stain manufactured by a reputable supplier and follow the firing instructions for satisfactory results. Copper oxide destroys cadmium/selenium glaze colour.

Chromium oxide, toxic: $\frac{1}{2}$ to 3 per cent will produce green in engobes and glazes. Produces red/orange in low-fired glazes with a high lead content. Combinations of 1 per cent chromium and 5 per cent tin will produce pink. In the presence of zinc, chromium will give various shades of brown.

Cobalt oxide, toxic: $\frac{1}{4}$–2 per cent produces blue in all glazes, engobes and clays. In lead glazes the colour is an inky blue and in alkaline glazes a brilliant blue. In the presence of magnesia the colour tends to purple. In high-fired magnesia glazes the purple blue may break up and produce red spots among the blue.

Cobalt carbonate, toxic: Sometimes preferred to the oxide form as the grain size is smaller, giving a more even distribution of colour in the glaze.

Copper oxide, toxic: 1–5 per cent produces green in most glazes, clays and engobes. In larger quantities it may produce a dense crystalline black. In alkaline glazes the colour tends to turquoise. The greater the proportion of alkaline flux and the smaller the proportion of alumina the more the turquoise will tend to a blue colour. Glazes incorporating barium as a flux may also become blue with the addition of copper. In reduction firing copper tends to give a red colour. The inclusion of tin (3 per cent) and iron ($\frac{1}{2}$ per cent) to copper ($\frac{1}{2}$–2 per cent) in an alkaline glaze with some borax will increase the chance of achieving the brightest example of this somewhat elusive colour. Matt glazes will give only muddy red colours.

Copper carbonate, toxic: Preferred to the oxide form for its finer grain but this is less vital in glazes than in engobes as the copper acts as a flux at all temperatures, and will disperse evenly in the glaze.

Crocus martis (purple iron): An impure iron ore producing mottled browns and yellows in stoneware glazes (see iron oxide for percentages).

Ilmenite: A combined form of iron and titanium oxides. 1–7 per cent is normally used to produce speckling of the colour in a glaze. Because of the iron content it produces a brown speckle when used on its own. It is often available in various grain sizes; the coarser the grain size the larger the coloured speckles.

Iron oxide (red iron, yellow iron, magnetic iron, purple iron): Probably the most commonly used colouring oxide. Lead earthenware glazes with 1–4 per cent of iron oxide will give yellow to amber, and 7 per cent will give dark brown. In alkaline glazes it will give brown. Lead glazes with small amounts of iron, 1 per cent together with tin 5 per cent or more, will produce a glaze which is cream with brown speckles.

Stoneware glazes containing felspar and whiting together with $\frac{1}{2}$–2 per cent of iron will give various shades of green when fired in a reducing atmosphere. If tin is included in the celadon glaze the resultant colour will be grey rather than green. 3–7 per cent of bone ash will encourage a blue-green colour in a light celadon glaze. 5–8 per cent of iron will produce brown tending to red in stoneware glazes and more than 10 per cent will, where the glaze is thickly applied, give black with red and brown on the edges of the form or where the glaze is thin. Glazes which have more than 10 per cent of iron may give a crystalline red surface in some reduction firings, particularly when applied over a red body.

Iron may be added to a glaze in the form of iron oxide (in various forms) or red clay. The latter is particularly common in stoneware glazes. Iron tends to find its way into most ceramic materials and reveals itself in the form of brown spots in glaze and body. While these iron inclusions in clay may be irritating they do not endanger the ware. The only exception is iron pyrites, which produces dense black spots when the clay is fired and black, slag-like pools if coated with glaze. The same material is responsible for the wide range of naturally coloured clays, ranging from yellow to dark brown when fired. Without long and careful milling it is impossible to achieve the yellow or red clay colour by adding iron to a white clay.

Magnetic iron produces speckled brown in glazes and clay and is used to produce iron crystals in crystalline glazes.

Manganese: 2–10 per cent may be used in glazes to produce brown in lead glaze or a purplish colour in alkaline glazes. The coarser types will produce a speckled colour in glazes and clays. Combined with small amounts of cobalt, the purple colour may become quite pronounced.

In stoneware glazes the resultant colour is brown rather than purple.

Nickel, toxic: 1–3 per cent will produce brown or green in glazes but is most commonly used to modify other colours. In stoneware glazes which contain zinc and particularly those which develop crystals the colour may be yellow, purple or blue.

Potassium bichromate, toxic: A form of chrome; 1–10 per cent is used to produce red and orange in high-lead glazes, fired below 1,000° C.

Rutile: A form of titanium and iron similar to ilmenite but containing less iron; used to produce speckling in glazes (2–10 per cent).

Selenium: See cadmium.

Tin: Up to 8 per cent will opacify a glaze and produce a white surface. More than this will tend to make most glazes crawl (see page 140).

Combined with chrome oxide, tin will produce pink. It is not melted by the glaze but is suspended in it, and tends to matt the glaze. This type of glaze is commonly used as a basis for overglaze decoration (see Chapter 18).

Titanium: 5–10 per cent will opacify and give a slightly matt surface to a glaze. The resultant colour is cream rather than the white of tin glazes. Pure titanium will produce a white opaque surface when added to a glaze. It may also be used to supply seed crystals in a crystal glaze.

Uranium: 1–10 per cent gives yellow and red in soft lead glazes, and yellow in stoneware glazes. If fired in a stoneware glaze reduction firing the colour will be a dull grey rather than yellow.

Vanadium, toxic: 5–10 per cent used to produce yellow in glazes, normally with the addition of tin.

Zirconium: Up to 15 per cent may be added to slips or glazes to produce a white, opaque surface. It is used in the place of tin in glazes containing chrome, to produce pale greens.

Some oxides do not fuse with the glaze to give an even dispersion of colour. It is advisable to grind or ball-mill all colouring additions, with a little of the glaze, unless a speckled colour is desired. Sieving of the glaze and then adding unsieved colouring material will increase the size of such speckles. This latter procedure can be adopted for heavy mottled effects but should be avoided if smooth-coloured glazes are required.

TEXTURE OF GLAZE SURFACES

A glaze may be shiny or matt in surface. An excess of alumina or calcium will produce a matt glaze, as will barium carbonate or zinc. In low-temperature glazes zinc or barium carbonate, between 10 and 20 per cent, will matt the glaze, but 25 per cent or more will be necessary in a boracic glaze.

In stoneware glazes similar amounts of zinc or barium carbonate may be used, or 40 per cent or more of whiting. The alumina content may be increased by the addition of china clay. When a matt surface is desired in an earthenware glaze, it is preferable to add equal proportions (4 per cent) of zinc, titanium and tin, which will give a semi-matt surface in most glazes fired at about 1,050° C.

Matt glazes may show a tendency to pinhole or crawl (see page 140). The ideal proportions for a particular glaze should be determined by experiment. All matt glazes are opaque. Because of their rough surface they are difficult to clean and are not in common use for tableware. Very matt glazes should not be confused with underfired glaze, and should be cooled slowly to produce good results.

Most metal oxides will act as glaze fluxes to some extent. A matt glaze may become shiny if coloured with sufficient metal oxides, notably copper, manganese and iron. It is advisable not to exceed a total of 10 per cent of metal oxide in a glaze recipe.

GLAZE TESTING

Most glazes should be tested before use, on small bisquited tiles or small pots, whichever is more convenient. It is essential to record the results of these tests carefully, so that the results may be repeated (or avoided) in the future. Duplicated test record forms will be found useful, with some such layout as this:

RECIPE

Fluxes   actual weight
%
%
%
%
%

Clay materials
%
%
%

Silica materials
%
%

            Total   100%

Matting agents
% of glaze
% of glaze

Colouring agents

% of glaze
% of glaze
% of glaze
% of glaze

Firing temperature
Firing time
Soaking time (if any)
Type of atmosphere (e.g. oxidation or reduction)

RESULTS

a Type of surface

b Colour

c Texture

Variations (if any)

a Thick application

b Thin application

c Vertical position

d Horizontal position

(*Above*) *Alice House Wall* by Robert Arneson, 1967. Polychromed earthenware sculpture, 72 in. × 96 in.

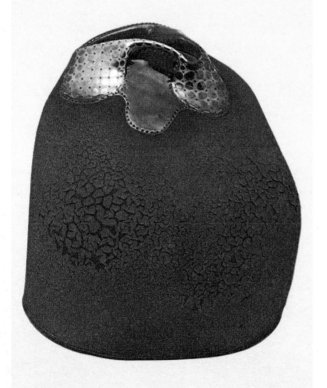

(*Left*) *Orange Form* by Ralph Bacerra, 1968. Earthenware sculpture with chrome and lead, metallic overglaze. Height 9 in.

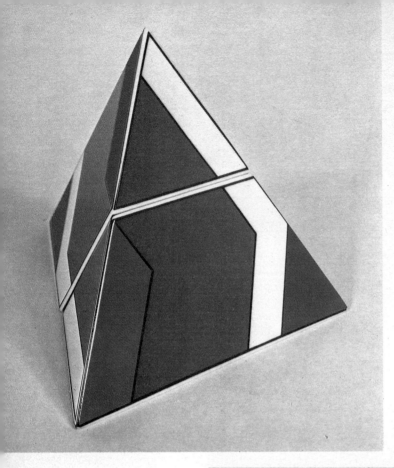

Two-piece Pyramid by G. Barton, 1972. Slip-cast bone china, ground to perfect shape after bisquit firing. White bone china glaze with on-glaze silk-screen transfer image.

Fixed emplacement teapot, by D. Hamilton, 1973. 10 in. high. Thrown body and spout, modelled knob and lugs, matt white oxidized stoneware glaze with body stains sprayed over the glaze through pierced metal grids. Aluminium base, aluminium and perspex handle.

16 Glaze application

A glaze is usually made up as a mixture of dry ingredients and water to produce a solution with the consistency of thin cream. Glazes may be formulated so that they can be applied to green clay, but normally the glaze is applied to clay which has been bisquited. The absorbent nature of the bisquit means that water is taken up by the form when it is immersed in the glaze solution, and the particles of glaze are thus bound to the surface of the clay.

Dipping

The commonest method of application is by 'dipping'. This method deposits an even layer of glaze all over the form and it requires no equipment other than a container large enough for the form to be totally immersed, if necessary.

Make up the glaze in sufficient quantity to provide an adequate depth of glaze in the chosen container. The glaze must be passed through a sieve of 200 mesh after being mixed with the water. If the glaze has been standing for several days it may be necessary to sieve the solution again before use. Testing the glaze by dipping several bisquited test pieces (which should, ideally, have been bisquited at the same temperature as the form to be glazed) will reveal any lumps in the solution and will indicate the length of time necessary to deposit a satisfactory depth of glaze. The glaze and water mixture should be of such consistency that when the form is immersed in it for five to ten seconds it will deposit a layer of glaze about one-sixteenth to one-eighth of an inch thick. The precise thickness of deposit may vary according to the type of glaze and the porosity of the bisquit. Some glazes are more suitable for thin application and others for thick. Some will give different kinds of colour or surface according to the thickness of the application.

To glaze the interior of a container form, pour the glaze inside, up to the top, hold it for a few seconds and then pour it out. Remove any dribbles immediately with a damp sponge and leave the form to dry. If no damp patches appear on the outside, glazing may be continued. Hold the form at the base and immerse it upside-down in the glaze. The air pressure will be sufficient to prevent the glaze from rising inside the form if there are no holes in the sides or base. One

Extruded column with slabbed base, by D. Hamilton. Matt white stoneware glaze applied by dipping each end several times, leaving the body exposed in the centre. Painted iron oxide image.

of the advantages of this method is that the interior and exterior may be coated with different glazes.

If the same glaze is to be applied to the interior and exterior, the form may be held in such a way that it can be swung into the glaze solution, so that it runs into and over the form simultaneously. Practice will be required to achieve a satisfactory glaze deposit.

In most dipping methods finger marks are produced which will show in the fired piece; alternatively, the glazing must be designed so that some of the form is deliberately left unglazed, and it may be held at this point during glazing. There are various devices which enable the form to be held and totally glazed with only small marks in the finished object. In industry finger-sleeves with hooks on the end are used, and the forms are dipped into the glaze held in these 'claws'. Any marks left on the dried form can be touched up with glaze before firing. A predetermined unglazed shape can be painted on the form in wax, and then the form can be held with the fingers on the waxed areas. In forms for stoneware firing it is quite common to leave one inch or more of the lower part of the form unglazed. The resultant surface is vitrified and can be a very satisfactory contrast to the glazed surface.

Pouring

The other common glazing technique in small workshops is to pour the glaze from a suitable jug so that it flows over the exterior. This will often create shapes on the form which may overlap and create secondary shapes. Several different glazes can be used to do this and the overlap areas may produce unexpected results. Overlapping glazes on test pieces

(*Below, left to right:*) glazing the interior of a form; dipping a form into glaze; holding the form to allow the excess glaze to drain away.

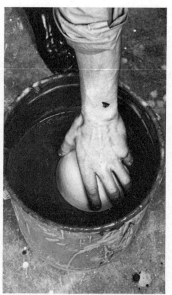

may be used as a preliminary to serious glaze testing. The interior of the form is glazed as with dipping but this should be completed and allowed to dry before glazing the exterior.

Spraying

This is another common method of applying glazes; the equipment required includes a compressor, an aerograph spray gun and a spray booth with an extractor fan. The compressor should provide a pressure of about thirty-five pounds per square inch. The gun is connected to the compressor by an airline so that when the air is forced through the gun it carries with it some of the liquid glaze, which is held in a cup container above the gun. The glaze-air mixture is forced from the gun and comes out in a cone-shaped spray.

The form to be glazed is placed on a turntable in the booth so that it may be easily rotated. The extractor is essential so that any glaze which is not sprayed onto the form will be drawn away from the operator and into the atmosphere outside. The form is sprayed with glaze by covering it with thin layers, gradually building up the required depth of glaze over all of the form rather than completing only one area at a time.

There is a tendency for the glaze to become atomized and produce a fluffy deposit of glaze which is very fragile and liable to be damaged when the form is being placed in the kiln. This type of glaze deposit has a very light bond with the bisquit and easily becomes dislodged when handled. As the glaze is not in the form of a complete skin there is an increased tendency for it to crawl when fired. It is therefore preferable to achieve a slightly wet surface on the form as it is sprayed, which is quite easily done by revolving the form slowly while keeping the spray not more than eighteen inches from the form.

Glazes of different colours may be sprayed to produce surfaces of different colours without hard edges between the colours. By using stencils held a few inches away from the form, more controlled shapes may be defined. Experiment will reveal countless variations of this technique.

Spraying is almost the only method of applying glaze to a large form, if an even all-over coating is required. It does not rely on the porosity of the bisquit to ensure adhesion of the glaze to the form so it is often used to reglaze fired surfaces which are unsatisfactory after the first firing, or if a two-glaze effect is required with carefully defined edges between them. If difficulty is experienced in getting the glaze to adhere to the glazed surface then the form may be heated – a hazardous process, but sometimes unavoidable. In no case should the form be heated beyond 80° C, otherwise it may crack when the cold air and glaze are sprayed upon it.

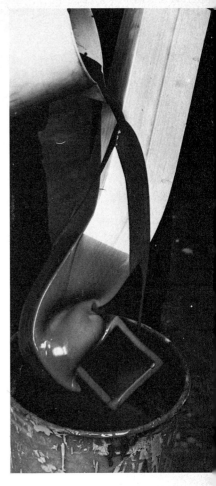

Pouring glaze over a form.

When preparing glaze for use in an aerograph it is most important to sieve the glaze through a 100-mesh sieve. If this is not done the glaze may include lumps which can block the gun and interrupt the glazing process. If the gun ceases to spray glaze when the trigger is squeezed, a quick method of unblocking the jet is to place a finger over the outlet so that the air is forced up into the cup and dislodges any blockage. This should be regarded as an emergency measure: the only real cure is to re-sieve the glaze.

Painting

Painting glaze onto bisquited forms should not entail any problems provided that the brushes are dense enough for sufficient glaze to be carried and produce a full brush-stroke. The porous clay will tend to suck the water from the brush immediately on contact and give uneven coverage, so this method is usually used to apply a contrasting glaze over one which has been applied all over the form. It is almost impossible to achieve a smooth surface of finished glaze by painting alone, for the brush will almost always leave a textured finish. It is, however, possible to get a fairly even layer of glaze if the glaze is banded onto the surface with the help of a banding wheel: the form is placed on the centre of the wheel and then slowly rotated while a fully loaded brush of glaze is held against the surface. Horizontal lines of glaze may be applied in this way, but some practice will be required before the novice will be able to apply a dense, even band.

A freer method of applying glazes may be found by flicking a fully loaded brush of glaze on to the surface and repeating this time and time again until the surface is completely covered with splashes of glaze. In this way several different glazes may be applied to a surface. This is a somewhat haphazard method but one that can produce very rich surfaces. It may be necessary to apply a preliminary coating of glaze to the surface to ensure that the form is completely covered, if this is necessary for the proper function of the piece.

Trailing

Glaze may also be applied with the slip trailer which is normally used to apply engobes to an unfired form. The technique is very similar to that of applying slip except that the glaze may have to be stiffened, if it has a tendency to run on a vertical surface, by either mixing the glaze with less water than usual or, if it is already mixed to the usual consistency, by heating it to drive off some of the water. With this technique it is possible to draw with the glaze, and to achieve interlacing effects when different-coloured glazes are used in combination. Again the form may be coated with a preliminary glaze if this is required.

(*Opposite, above*) Spraying glaze on a form, using a compressor, spray gun and extractor booth.

(*Opposite*) Spraying glaze on an object too large to fit into an extractor booth. The working area is well ventilated and the operator is protected from the atomized glaze by goggles and a respirator.

Sgraffito

Once the glaze or glazes have been applied lines may be scratched through the unfired glaze so that the body is revealed when the glaze has been fired. These lines can then be filled with a contrasting glaze or left unglazed. As the glaze is dry at this stage there will be a tendency for lines with chittered edges to be produced. This may not matter if the glaze is a fairly liquid type as the edge will soften during firing, but if it is a matt glaze there will be an increased tendency to crawl, or for pieces to fall away from the form as the adhesion of the glaze to the body is lessened. It is very rare that a satisfactory repair can be effected and it is quicker to wash off the glaze and start again, or accept the result and refire with another glaze.

Application faults

The three most common faults are: *Glaze applied too thinly* owing to too much water in the glaze solution or saturation of the form with water after glazing the interior. Avoid weak glaze solutions and ensure that the glaze is well stirred, to disperse the glaze powder, before use. Thin or very porous forms should be dried after glazing one surface. *Runs or dribbles* due to careless glazing: when they are dry, pare these away with a sharp knife or rub them off gently with the fingers. *Patchy glazing* is caused by careless handling of the bisquit clay. If the form is left for long periods after bisquiting, dust can settle on the surface and act as a resist during glazing. Excessive handling can deposit oil and grease on the clay with similar results.

17 Glaze firing

While it may be assumed that the only difference between high- and low-temperature firing will be the final temperature, this is far from true. The method of packing and firing during the initial period will vary according to the type of glaze being fired and the temperature which will be finally achieved.

EARTHENWARE GLAZES

These glazes are usually fired in an oxidizing atmosphere or a neutral one. It is, therefore, in order that the objects be closely packed, but the space between one form and another should not be less than a quarter of an inch. If the form is glazed all over the outer surface it will be necessary to support it on a stilt, so that when the glaze starts to soften and melt it will not bond the form to the shelf. While it may be possible to separate such an amalgam of shelf and form should it occur, it is rare that this can be done without damage to one or the other. Unnecessary loss of expensive shelving should be avoided, as indeed should needless damage to the work being fired.

Instead of spurs and stilts, sand is sometimes used to support complex forms but this can only be done where the form is unglazed on the base as the sand will stick to any glazed surface. Sand should be used with care in kilns where the draught of the fire may blow the sand onto other glazed forms.

STONEWARE GLAZES

Spurs and stilts normally soften at temperatures above $1,180°$ C and should not be used in stoneware firings. Forms for stoneware firing should be unglazed where they rest on the kiln shelves.

As most clays will soften to some extent at $1,200°$ C and above, shelves for this type of firing should be treated on one side only with commercial bat wash, which will prevent the forms sticking to the shelves. Shelves treated with bat wash should not be placed with the washed surface on the underside as there is a danger that some of the wash may fall from the shelf on to the glazed forms beneath it.

Once the ware has been packed – and this must be done with care, rather than quickly – the heat may be induced according to the type of kiln (Simmerstat 50, three-way switch 'medium' setting, gas kiln burners half on) so that the temperature will rise at about 100° C per hour. The alpha/beta change will occur again at 745° C and this temperature must be passed slowly to ensure an even expansion of the quartz throughout the object. Beyond this temperature the heat may be induced at the most convenient rate. The type of kiln being used will determine the rate of 'full power' climb in temperature (e.g. Simmerstat 100, three-way switch 'high' setting, gas kiln burners on full). The final temperature may be followed by a 'soak' if necessary, to give a satisfactory glaze surface. Too long a soak will cause the glaze to become too liquid and perhaps run off the form even when the correct thickness of glaze has been applied. It may also produce glossy glazes where matt glazes are expected, or even have the effect of fixing the glazed form onto any spur or stilt which may have been placed under it. To avoid this the glaze should be pared away where it makes contact with the stilt. Whether or not a soak is required must be determined by experiment.

Once the top temperature has been reached it is essential to cool the glaze satisfactorily. If the glaze is to have a matt finish it will be necessary to cool it slowly in order to induce devitrification of the glaze. During this cooling the crystals which give the glaze its matt surface will form: without sufficient time to develop, these crystals will remain very small and produce a surface less matt than that which may have been expected. Normally the cooling period will last from the maturing temperature of the glaze until it has cooled to 200° C lower, taking about four hours at a cooling rate of 50° C per hour. With some kilns, which lose heat rapidly when the fuel is cut off, owing to inadequate insulation, it may be found necessary to maintain some heat input to prevent too rapid a cooling of the glazes. On electric kilns, reducing the power input to about half will have the effect of bringing down the temperature at a rate of 50° C per hour when the top temperature exceeds 1,000° C. With gas kilns the amount of fuel needed to reduce the temperature at the desired rate will have to be determined by experiment, but closing all the air inlets and the chimney damper is normally sufficient to ensure that the kiln cools slowly.

Regardless of the rate of cooling necessary for a satisfactory glaze surface, the glaze may be cooled at the normal rate of 100° C per hour when it falls below the hardening point – the point at which a glaze hardens to a solid glass, usually 200° C below its maturing temperature. Ideally, the glaze should be allowed to cool to room temperature at

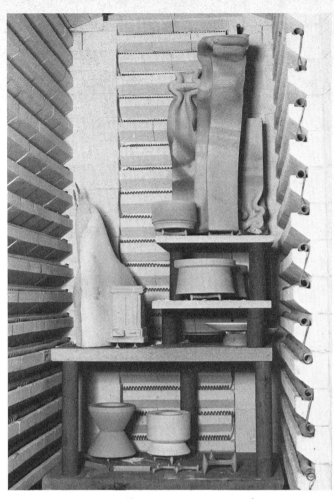

A kiln packed with forms coated with earthenware glazes; they are supported on stilts and saddles.

A stoneware gloss packing for firing.

this rate but more slowly past the alpha/beta changes (see page 118); usually the kiln door is eased open at about 100° C as the cooling from this temperature to about room temperature is naturally quite slow.

GREEN GLAZES (once-fired glazes)

In the case of green glazes – those which are applied to clay before it has been bisquit-fired – the initial stage of the firing is controlled as if it were a bisquit firing (see page 115) and the kiln should be heated with the ventilation bung removed. Once the maturing point of the glaze has been attained the kiln should be cooled according to the needs of the glaze.

VARIATIONS IN KILN ATMOSPHERE

Those kilns in which no burning takes place, i.e. muffle and electric kilns, will always have a neutral or oxidizing atmosphere in which the colours and surfaces produced will be fairly constant and predictable. While this is an advantage in most cases, there may be occasions when a reduction atmosphere will be desired and this must be induced artificially. Such action usually has the effect of damaging the elements of an electric kiln (see page 34) and is to be avoided whenever possible, though in some electric kilns provision is made for reduction by the use of silicon carbide elements. The atmosphere within muffle kilns or any other non-burning type can be reduced by the introduction into the kiln, accidentally or deliberately, of some matter which will burn.

Many different substances have been used to achieve satisfactory reduction, from various types of wood to naphthalene in the form of moth balls, but the commonest method in studios is to introduce town or natural gas into the kiln by means of a gas poker inserted through the spy-hole. This is quite safe if the poker is turned off until it is in the kiln.

With burning kilns of the semi-muffle type reduction can easily be achieved by the closing of the secondary air inlets and partially closing the chimney damper. With home-made and early stoneware kilns reduction is the usual atmosphere produced during firing as it is often difficult to introduce enough air into the kiln chamber to allow the flames to burn without drawing upon the oxygen in the clay and colouring oxides. If the flames in a burning type of kiln are very long, and reach into the flue, it is almost certain that the atmosphere inside the chamber is of the reduction variety. They may be caused by the flue being too effective, i.e. drawing too strongly, or by too little air passing through the air-gas inlets and not allowing the fuel time to burn completely.

The timing of the reduction is a matter for preference rather than any absolute criteria. Some ceramists prefer stoneware glazes to be reduced starting at about 1,100° C, continuing the reduction until the maturing temperature of the glaze has been reached. The atmosphere is allowed to stabilize itself during cooling. Others prefer to reduce the atmosphere from just below the maturing temperature and this is maintained as the kiln cools by continuing to burn the fuel and sealing the kiln, so that there can be no possibility of any air leaking into the firing chamber. Some ceramists reduce their kilns intermittently, others keep the reduction constant during either the heating or the cooling. Each type of fuel, each type of kiln, each type of method of reduction will have particular qualities which may be researched and tested.

Localized reduction may be achieved in an otherwise oxidizing kiln by adding a small amount (up to 10 per cent) of silicon carbide to the glaze, or by placing the form to be reduced in a saggar together with a reducing agent such as wood ash, sealing the saggar and firing the kiln in the usual way.

Earthenware, stoneware and porcelain may be reduced but the most common reduction firings are for the two latter, together with non-commercial lustres.

In stoneware and porcelain firings, especially those which are to be reduced, great care must be taken in the packing of the forms in the kiln, as kiln furniture has a tendency to soften during this type of firing. If the shelves are loaded with forms which are too heavy, not only will the shelving be irrevocably damaged but there is a good chance that the stacked forms and shelves may move so that they touch each other; even worse, the moving stack may set up a 'domino' reaction with other stacks and most of the work will be ruined.

With earthenware and bisquit firings three props may be sufficient for each shelf but a stoneware or porcelain firing may need four.

Those kilns which are designed to pass the flames through the stacks of forms must be packed according to the manufacturer's specifications to ensure that the heating of the kiln is as even as possible. In the case of reduction firing it is important that there is plenty of room round the forms, so that the changing atmosphere will have every opportunity to have full effect in every part of the kiln. To test the progress of a firing it is helpful to set, in a convenient place for easy withdrawal by means of a long metal rod, some test pieces in the shape of rings, so that as the firing proceeds the rings may be withdrawn to check the melting of the glaze and the degree of reduction (if any).

Under reduction conditions, most kilns will build up pressure inside the chamber. When a bung is removed, to

The stoneware glaze firing completed (with the accidental collapse of one piece). The pyrometric cones have been softened by the heat and indicate the maximum temperature achieved during the firing.

inspect the forms or to withdraw test rings, a long flame may come through the hole. Care must be taken to avoid accidental, and sometimes serious, burning to the operator's face.

GLAZE UNPACKING

Before unpacking a glaze kiln it is essential to ensure that the temperature has fallen to a point where the glaze and clay will not receive a thermal shock when coming into contact with air at normal room temperature, i.e. below 100° C.

The unpacking of a glaze firing will vary according to the complexity of the packing and the temperature to which the kiln has been fired. If the objects have been supported on stilts during the firing, there will be at least some small spurs of stilt attached to the underneath of the form. These spurs are very sharp and great care must be taken to avoid deep cuts. The forms should be removed from the kiln and the stilts detached by tapping them gently with a sorting tool. Even if a stilt comes away by itself when the form is removed from the kiln, there may still be small, razor-sharp pieces of spur, almost invisible but still dangerous.

Stilts which have been used once should be inspected to see whether they can be reused. A stilt should be thrown away if one of its arms is broken, or if a point is so badly damaged that it will not present a sharp edge or point when supporting another form. There is nothing more irritating than sorting through a box of damaged stilts to find one useful one.

Just as the stilts may leave spurs on the fired objects, they may also leave them on the kiln shelving. This is a considerable hazard as shelving may be subject to a good deal of handling by different people. All shelving should be cleaned by passing a metal ruler across each surface to remove any unnoticed spurs. If the glaze has run off a form and spotted the shelving, this may be removed with a sorting tool and then with a steel ruler.

If the forms have been stacked without stilts, or if the glaze has run over the stilts in a deep curtain, the form will probably be held immovable on the shelf. Removing such an amalgam of form and glaze is very difficult, but the usual decision is to sacrifice the shelf in order to preserve the object. The first release method to try is to immerse the whole mass in water and chip round the junction of glaze and shelf. The water may seep under the glaze and help it to separate from the shelf. In any case the water will soften the shock of the chipping, which may otherwise break the form.

Obviously prevention is better than cure: careful glazing and proper packing and firing will help to avoid the worst results of such accidents.

Always replace props and shelves so that they can be easily found when the time comes for the next packing. If the shelves are clean and the props sorted by size, the packing of the kiln is much less frustrating, and energy can be devoted to proper and safe packing of the ware.

18 On-glaze decoration

From time to time it may be necessary or desirable to reglaze an already glazed form, or to paint a graphic image on the surface. The main problem in trying to get a glaze onto an already glazed surface is that the fired glaze has rendered the form impervious to water. Dipping or pouring a fresh glaze over the surface will have little or no effect as it will run over the form leaving little or no deposit of glaze. One of the ways to overcome this problem is to heat the form in a kiln to about 80° C – with care, to avoid putting undue strain on the form and the glaze – and then to dip it in the glaze solution. It is not possible to double-dip a second glaze over this because the underglaze will be washed off.

The only way to build up a dense layer of glaze is to heat up the form and spray the glaze on with an aerograph. There may be a tendency for the fresh glaze to start to run as it is applied and the form cools down, but if the sprayed layers are kept thin, so that as the form is turned there is time for it to dry before another layer is sprayed over it, there should be sufficient bite for subsequent layers to adhere. Very rich effects can be achieved by overglazing. The glaze which has been fired first will require more heat to melt it than if it were being fired for the first time. It is of course possible to wax-resist other designs on the fired glaze before applying the second glaze. It is also possible to paint oxides over the unfired second glaze. The exact reactions of any glaze to all these techniques will have to be determined by experiment.

One other method which can be used to good effect is to put a stoneware glaze over an earthenware-glazed form and fire it to stoneware temperature (if the clay will stand it). If the form is stoneware-glazed, earthenware glaze may be put over it and fired either to earthenware or to stoneware temperature. Take the precaution of placing the form on a soft-fired clay pad so that if the glaze runs uncontrollably off the form it will collect on the pad and not come into contact with the kiln shelves.

Painting on fired glaze

If it is desired to paint colouring pigment onto fired glaze the problem is similar to that encountered with reglazing: the glazed surface is impervious so it is necessary to mix the colouring pigment with something which will increase its stickiness, to prevent it from running as it is painted onto the surface. Mixing the colour with gum arabic will usually suffice.

As with all glazing and painting, great care must be taken to ensure that no part of the painted or glazed surface is dislodged, as it is almost impossible to repair any damage without an ugly mark being left by what appears, in the unfired state, to be a perfect match.

ENAMELS

Enamels may be described as low-temperature glazes; they are usually applied on top of glazes which have been fired to a higher temperature. While it is possible to compound enamels in the studio, it is a lengthy process. Enamels are available from several manufacturers, in various hues and tones, and there have been substantial efforts to improve the safety of these colours in recent years. Until recently lead was a vital fluxing ingredient in most enamels, but as the temperature to which enamels are fired is usually quite low, there is a great risk that the lead in the enamel will be released into any slightly acid liquid with which it may come into contact; such a lead solution would be harmful to anyone who might consume it.

Most enamel colours now available from ceramic colour manufacturers comply with the stringent government safety regulations, but mixing and firing instructions should always be observed. Every precaution should be taken to ensure that, while handling unfired enamels, none is accidentally consumed.

Enamels may be applied to either a glazed or a bisquit surface but for a full colour reaction, and one that closely resembles the manufacturer's colour samples, they should be applied to smooth, white, fired glaze. On bisquited surfaces enamels will produce thin and rather patchy colours.

They can be painted, sprayed or ground-laid onto the form. Painting requires considerable skill to achieve satisfactory results. In the industry, a period of apprenticeship is required before an enamel painter is considered to be sufficiently skilled to proceed to production ware, but simple designs can be produced in the studio with a little practice. The enamel is supplied in the form of a powder which can be mixed with a suitable oil medium according to the chosen method of application. Certain oils may require special thinners but normally turpentine is used.

Tools: muller and slab, palette-knife, brushes. Enamel for painting may be mixed with one of the several oils which are sold for this purpose. Grind the enamel powder with the chosen oil on a palette of glass or a glazed tile, using a palette-knife or a muller. The resultant mixture should be smooth and free of lumps, and the oil should make it possible to paint the mixture on a glazed surface without any dribbles or raised brushmarks. If the mixture runs, the oil is too thin or too much thinners has been added. Brushes should be of the finest-quality sable, or those sold especially for enamelling. Stencils or other devices may be used. All tools should be cleaned with white spirit after use.

Sprayed enamel is usually mixed with 1 per cent starch and enough water to bring it to the consistency of cream. The mixture should be sieved through a 250-mesh lawn. A special spray gun with a fine jet should be used, and the air pressure adjusted to the manufacturer's specification.

The sprayed enamel should be built up in thin layers but the over-all thickness should not exceed two millimetres: if it is any thicker than this the enamel may peel off the form when fired. An air brush can be used to make thin lines of sprayed enamel, but before this or any spraying technique is used on a piece of work it is advisable to practise by spraying ink on paper, instead of enamel on glaze.

Stencils can be used but it may be necessary to fix the stencil to the glazed surface, for which adhesive tape is usually suitable. It is also possible to sgraffito through the enamel but there is a tendency for the edge of the scratch to be chittered, which may be a considerable disadvantage in producing some types of image.

Ground laying

This is an industrial technique in which the glazed surface of the object is first covered with ground-laying oil. When this oil has dried to the extent that, when it is brushed with a finger, it makes a squeaking sound, it should be buffed with a silk boss filled with cotton wool. This bossing or patting down removes any brushmarks and levels off the oil surface. The enamel powder is then dusted onto the oil and if the procedure has been correctly followed the enamel will stick to the oil in an even, dense layer. This technique should be used with care: there is a real danger that some of the enamel dust may be inhaled during the dusting operation, and the operation should therefore be carried out inside an extractor booth. If the oil has been applied too thickly there is a possibility that it will run when warmed during firing.

The other main use of enamel is in the silk-screen or lithographic transfer process. It is not within the scope of this book to describe this technique in detail. Very simply, the enamel is printed onto a transfer paper and then covered with a layer of gum. When this layer has dried, the paper and image are soaked in water so that the transfer paper is released from the printed image and gum. The gum with the image fixed to it can be lifted out of the water, placed on the glazed surface and pressed down so that it sticks to the form. When the transfer is fired the gum burns away, leaving an enamel image bonded to the form. Photographic images can be reproduced in this way.

Firing enamels

If the enamel has been applied with an oil medium, the firing should be very slow in the initial stages so that the oil is driven off very slowly. Smoke will come from the kiln at this stage and in electric kilns the ventilating bung should be removed.

Any crazing which may have occurred in the glaze firing will become very obvious, as the enamel will flow into these hairline cracks to produce a coloured network.

Enamels are usually fired to between 720° and 750° C in an oxidizing atmosphere.

LUSTRES

Lustres are similar to enamels in that they are low-fired but, as the name suggests, they produce metallic surfaces. Traditionally, lustres are fired in a reduction atmosphere. Industrially manufactured lustres are supplied suspended in a suitable medium together with a reduction agent, so that when fired in a neutral or oxidizing atmosphere the metallic surface is produced without changing the kiln atmosphere. The colouring agent is a metallic salt. While manufactured lustres are simple to use and fire, they do not produce the richness and variety of those compounded in the traditional way. The criterion to apply to a manufactured colour is that the results should be of an assured quality and of a greater dependability than the more elusive and variable studio colour.

Manufactured lustres are fired at about 750° C. Most lustres will produce the expected surface when painted on a shiny glazed surface, but if the glaze is slightly matt, a silver lustre may produce a grey gunmetal surface rather than a silver. Cheap gold is glossy, but good-quality gold (burnishing gold) will produce, when fired, a dull surface until it is burnished or polished with either a spun-glass burnisher or a soft cloth and burnishing sand. This has the effect of removing the scum on the surface, to reveal the gold surface. Many different coloured lustres are commercially available.

19 Special ceramics

RAKU

Raku is a glaze-firing process. Briefly it may be described as a bisquit-fired ceramic form on which the glaze firing is carried out very quickly in a preheated kiln. This process may be carried out at stoneware temperatures, but it is more usually done at between 900° and 950° C.

The clay used to make forms which are to be fired by the raku process must be coarse and include a large proportion of grog, so that it may withstand the thermal shock of being placed in the preheated kiln. A coarse fireclay with grog added is the commonest type of body and is available ready mixed from some clay suppliers; it may be coloured by the addition of red clay or metal oxides. Because of this coarse texture it may be painful to throw forms in this body but any of the other hand methods of forming it can be used. The section of the clay form should be as even as possible so that it may absorb the heat of the kiln rapidly, evenly and without cracking and lose it as easily when suddenly cooled.

Forms of raku should not be very large (maximum six inches in any dimension) so that they can be handled easily; also, larger pieces tend to dunt.

A glaze for raku (which may be coloured with suitable metal oxides) usually contains a high proportion (up to 70 per cent) of lead and is fired at 950° C. When the clay forms have been bisquited and cooled normally they may be glazed. The glaze should be quite heavily applied to produce good results, and the forms placed near the kiln or on top of it so that they may dry thoroughly before being fired.

Firing raku

A pair of long-handled tongs will be necessary, together with asbestos mittens, to facilitate the safe placement and removal of the form from the hot kiln. The kiln should be heated up to 1,000° C whilst empty. To avoid damage to the kiln by glaze running off the form it is advisable to put small clay tiles on the floor where the forms are to be placed.

When this temperature has been reached and the glazed forms dried, take one form, holding it firmly in the tongs. Then open the door of the kiln and place the form carefully inside. Obviously this must be done quickly to avoid excessive loss of heat when the door is opened. The glaze will take ten to fifteen minutes to melt, and this can be observed through a convenient spyhole.

When the glaze has fluxed, remove the form and place another in the kiln. It will be observed that the glaze goes through a fierce boiling stage before settling into a fully fluxed state. Borax boils for a long time before fluxing and is unsuitable alone for raku glazes unless a very broken surface is required.

Fuel must be supplied to the kiln throughout this process, and in the case of electric kilns it is important to see that the power is switched off during the time the door is open if no automatic cut-off device is fitted.

Cooling the glaze

The form when removed from the kiln will have a coating of molten glaze, which will harden as the form cools in the atmosphere. During this cooling time the colour of the form may be changed by different atmospheric conditions. The commonest method, apart from leaving it near the kiln to cool slowly (in which case it will produce oxidized results), is to place the hot form in a container full of sawdust, which must be kept damp to prevent it bursting into flames. The heat of the form will ignite the sawdust immediately around it and if it is left to cool this will have characteristic reduction effects, i.e. light-coloured clays will have blackened surfaces where there is no glaze. Colour will be determined by the presence of metal oxides, if any are present (see Chapter 15).

Raku glazes are often crazed because of the sudden change in temperature to which they are exposed. The forms may be reheated and reglazed several times using different glazes, or oxide can be rubbed into the craze marks.

Japanese raku tea bowl. Hand-formed cup fired by the raku process.

Because raku forms are usually low-fired with high-lead glazes they are potentially poisonous: food or drink should never be contained in vessels coated with this type of glaze. The rapidity of the low-temperature firing may produce ware which is fragile, but raku results can be very exciting and it is a means of demonstrating some aspects of ceramics in a dramatic way.

EGYPTIAN PASTE

Egyptian paste is a type of body which the Egyptians are believed to have used in the manufacture of jewelry and small tomb figures. It has the characteristic of containing within it soluble fluxes sufficient to develop its own glaze when dried and fired.

The fluxes are dissolved in the physically combined water. As the clay dries, and the water evaporates, the fluxes are deposited on the clay surface in the form of a fragile crust of crystals. The clay is fired to 950° C approximately, and when cool the fluxes are found to have fused with the free silica in the body to form a glaze.

Poor deposits of glaze in the finished object can normally be attributed either to dislodgement of the fragile crust during handling and packing in the kiln, or to a too rapid rise in temperature during the early stages of firing, and steam blowing the crust off the clay surface.

One other problem is that the clay glazes itself on every surface and care must be taken to stilt the form in the kiln,

English Nottingham salt-glazed stoneware mug, 1771. Moulded form with sprigged and drawn design.

English Staffordshire salt-glazed pew group, c. 1730. Slabbed base and back, folded slabs for the figures, with modelled details.

or to place sand beneath it to prevent it sticking to the shelf. It is sometimes possible to remove the crust from the base of the form before firing without damaging the rest of the surface.

Because of the pure alkaline nature of the flux, copper when present will give blue, and other oxides (in particular cobalt and manganese) will produce rich colours; the colouring oxides may be introduced into the clay or painted on the glaze. Several clays of different hues are quite commonly used in forms made from Egyptian paste.

Because of its sandy texture this clay is difficult to model and is suitable only for small objects (four inches in any dimension). A convenient method of forming it is to press it into moulds of plaster or bisquited clay.

SALT GLAZING

This type of glaze, commonly found on drain- and sewer-pipes, was one of the first types of stoneware glazes used in Europe, and originated in Germany. The glaze is characterized by an orange-peel texture and the colour depends on the metal oxides present in the clay. The process, which is simple, consists of firing the clay forms to the maturing point of the body (usually 1,250° C plus) and then throwing salt into the kiln. The salt vaporizes to produce a sodium vapour which combines with the free silica in the body to form a glaze. The exact amount of salt necessary to produce a rich glaze must be determined by experiment, and will depend upon the volume and firing characteristic of the kiln.

The inside of the kiln becomes coated with sodium glaze, which vaporizes with every firing, so that gradually less salt is required to produce the desired thickness of glaze. For the same reason every firing will produce salt glaze upon the ware and it is advisable to find a kiln already used for salt glazing, or to reserve one kiln for that purpose only, rather than hope to produce normal stoneware glazes in subsequent firings. Salt glazing gives off toxic vapours and is best done outside the studio.

Appendix 1 : workshop procedure

EQUIPMENT

All equipment is potentially dangerous and should be used only after receiving proper instructions.

Do not force clay into pugmills by hand or with the aid of pieces of wood. Before attending to the maintenance or repair of equipment, ensure that it is insulated from the mains supply.

Always check that an electric kiln is switched off on all switches before opening the door. Gas kilns should have the mains valve and individual burner taps turned off after use, and checked before starting the ignition procedure.

Manufacturers provide guidelines and instructions on the use and maintenance of equipment. Make sure that you are familiar with these.

Wear dark glasses when viewing the interior of a red-hot kiln.

MATERIALS

Store plastic clay in a damp store if possible. Dry materials should, where possible, be stored outside the workshop area in airtight containers and marked with secure and legible labels. Many materials have similar appearances; confusion can be expensive and dangerous.

Keep colouring compounds well separated from clay and glaze materials.

Keep plaster isolated from the main workshop area.

HYGIENE

Do not handle glaze materials unless absolutely necessary: use ladles and scoops where practicable.

Keep a first-aid kit handy. Clean and protect all wounds and scratches with waterproof dressings as soon as possible.

Use soap, nailbrush and a clean towel after making and applying glaze.

Use a barrier cream if your hands become sore after constant exposure to water.

Clean your workshop regularly.

Do not drink from workshop bowls or jugs.

Do not eat, drink or smoke while you are working.

Have regular health checks for heavy-metal release if lead or cadmium compounds are used in the workshop.

Appendix 2: useful information

MATERIAL IN SOLUTION

The amount of solid material in a solution, e.g. the amount of glaze material suspended in water, can be expressed as

$$D - 20 \times \frac{G}{G-1}$$

where D = the weight of one pint of solution.

G = the specific gravity of the solid.

Example:

Solution of clay and water equalling 36 oz per pint.

$D = 36$ oz.

$G = 2{\cdot}6$ (common for most clay minerals).

$$36 - 20 \times \frac{2{\cdot}6}{2{\cdot}6-1} \text{ oz.} = 16 \times 1{\cdot}625 = 26 \text{ oz.}$$

The solution contains 26 oz. of dry material.

And to add 5% of colouring agent to one pint of the solution

$$\frac{26}{100} \times 5 \text{ oz. should be added, i.e. } 1{\cdot}3 \text{ oz.}$$

PLASTER OF PARIS

Probable plaster/water proportions, for plaster of paris moulds:

1lb. 14 oz. plaster to 1 pint of water, or

3lb. 12 oz. plaster to 2 pints of water.

In other words, weight for weight the proportions should be

3:2 plaster:water.

PYROMETRIC CONES

Seger Cones. At 150° C per hour temperature rise:

cone no.	018	melts at	705° C	014	melts at	820° C
	017		730	013		850
	016		755	012		870
	015		780	011		890

cone no. 010	melts at	910° C	3a	melts at	1,170° C
09		935	4a		1,195
08		955	5a		1,215
07		970	6a		1,240
06		990	7		1,260
05		1,000	8		1,280
04		1,025	9		1,300
03		1,055	10		1,320
02		1,085	11		1,340
01		1,105	12		1,370
1a		1,125	13		1,410
2a		1,150	14		1,435

Orton cones. At 150° C per hour temperature rise:

cone no. 018	melts at	725° C	02	melts at	1,115° C
017		765	01		1,145
016		785	1		1,160
015		805	2		1,165
014		830	3		1,170
013		855	4		1,190
012		870	5		1,205
011		890	6		1,230
010		905	7		1,250
09		930	8		1,260
08		955	9		1,285
07		995	10		1,305
06		1,015	11		1,325
05		1,045	12		1,337
04		1,075	13		1,349
03		1,100	14		1,398

COLOUR WITHIN A KILN DURING FIRING

TEMPERATURE (° C)	COLOUR	FIRED WARE
500	dull red	
750	red	enamels
1,000	bright red	bisquit and earth-
1,100	orange red	enware glaze
1,150	bright orange	high bisquit
1,200	white orange	stoneware; bone-
1,300	white	china bisquit
1,350	blue white	porcelain

PROPORTIONAL SHRINKAGE OF CLAY FORMS

Wet to dry   loses 1 part in 15

     to earthenware   1 part in 12

     to stoneware   1 part in 10

     to porcelain   1 part in 8

Note: These figures are approximate; they will vary slightly from one clay to another.

BASIC GLAZES

Earthenware (1,060° C)

     lead bisilicate 80%

     china clay   20%

     For white, add up to 8% tin oxide; for black, add 4% manganese oxide, 2% cobalt and 2% iron oxide. To matt, add 10% zinc; for satin finish, add 4% zinc oxide, 4% tin oxide and 4% titanium oxide.

Alkaline glaze

     use a commercial glaze or frit.

Low-solubility glaze (safe for tableware)

     use a commercial glaze, but do not add copper oxide as a colorant.

Stoneware (1,280° C)

Matt white

     felspar   50%

     dolomite   22·5%

     whiting   3·5%

     china clay   24%

     (add 5% tin oxide if necessary, for whiteness)

Transparent

     felspar   70%

     whiting   12·5%

     china clay   13%

     flint   4·5%

     (for black, add 10% iron oxide)

Calcium matt

felspar	20%
whiting	22%
dolomite	15%
zinc	3%
flint	40%

(shiny where thinly applied)

Appendix 3 : some suppliers in Britain and the USA

GENERAL
L.H.Butcher & Co., 3628 E Olympic Boulevard, San Francisco, California.
Ferro Corporation, 4130 East 56th Street, Cleveland, Ohio.
Harrison Mayer Ltd, Meir, Stoke on Trent.
W. Podmore & Sons, Caledonian Mills, Shelton, Stoke on Trent.
Wengers Ltd, Etruria, Stoke on Trent.

COLOURS
Blyth Colour Works, Cresswell, Stoke on Trent.

LUSTRES
Johnson Matthey & Co. Ltd, 73 Hatton Garden, London E.C.1 (and many branch offices).

KILNS
A.D. Alpine Inc., 353 Coral Circle, El Segunda, California.
British Ceramic Services Co. Ltd, Bricesco House, Wolstanton, Newcastle-under-Lyme, Staffordshire.
Gibbons Bros Ltd, P.O. Box 20, Brierley Hill, Staffordshire.
Kilns and Furnaces, Keele Street, Tunstall, Stoke on Trent.

WHEELS AND EQUIPMENT
W. Boulton & Co., Burslem, Stoke on Trent.
Denver Fireclay Co., Denver, Colorado.
Edwards & Jones, Longton, Stoke on Trent.

CLAY
Acme Marls Ltd, Clough Street, Hanley, Stoke on Trent.
Kentucky-Tennessee Clay Co., Mayfield, Ohio.
Pike Bros., Wareham, Dorset.
Potclays, Wharf House, Copeland Street, Hanley, Stoke on Trent.

KILN FURNITURE
Acme Marls Ltd, Clough Street, Hanley, Stoke on Trent.
J.D. Craig (Agents), Readi Sales Co., P.O. Box 653, Trenton, New Jersey.
Diamond Refractories Ltd, Hartshill, Stoke on Trent.

Glossary

A shelf or carrying board, specifically a kiln shelf.	BAT
A refractory material which prevents melting clay or glaze from sticking to the kiln shelves.	BAT WASH
The state of clay when fired but unglazed.	BISQUIT
The deformation of a form where either the clay has started to boil or air trapped in the form has expanded during firing.	BLOAT
A mixture of clays and other materials producing a workable material suitable for manufacturing processes.	BODY
A mechanical device carrying a mixture of liquid or vapour, fuel and air from which the mixture flows and burns.	BURNER
The process of smoothing and polishing clay or lustre to produce a glossy surface.	BURNISHING
The space between particles of clay, occupied by water before firing and decreasing in size as firing of the clay proceeds.	CAPILLARY
The process of forming clay in a mould.	CASTING
A retaining wall which determines the outer shape of a mould during its manufacture.	COTTLE
The method of joining one piece of clay to another by scoring (cross-hatching) the two surfaces and bonding them together with a solution of clay and water (slurry).	CROSS-HATCH AND SLURRY
A material or combination of materials which prevents clay particles from sticking together.	DEFLOCCULANT
The crystallization of some glass-forming material during the cooling of a glaze.	DEVITRIFICATION
A test piece or ring, placed in the kiln so that it may be moved during the firing to assess progress and atmospheric conditions within the kiln.	DRAW TRIAL
See Deflocculant.	ELECTROLYTE
A slip which is applied over a clay to change the colour of the form.	ENGOBE
The ability of two or more materials, when combined, to melt at a temperature lower than the melting-point of either of the separate materials.	EUTECTIC
The cleaning of rough or untidy clay or glazed edges before or after firing.	FETTLING

FIRING	The process of exposing clay and glazes to controlled heat within the kiln.
FIT	The relationship between the thermal expansion of a glaze and that of the body.
FLUX	A material which will cause other materials to melt at reduced temperatures.
FREE SILICA	That silica in a clay body which does not form part of the clay particles and is therefore free to change its crystalline form when heated.
FRIT	Several materials combined by heating to produce a safe and convenient single material.
GEL	The quality of a slip which does not drain evenly from a mould.
GLOSS	The firing of glaze upon clay forms.
GONE OFF	The state of plaster of paris which, having been mixed with water, has set hard, become heated and then cooled.
GREEN CLAY	Clay which is unfired.
GROG	Fired and crushed clay, added to unfired clay to coarsen its texture and decrease its shrinkage.
HEAT WORK	The relationship between time and temperature which promotes certain reactions in ceramics and permits their development to the desired stage.
KIDNEY	A rubber or steel smoothing tool shaped like a kidney.
LAMINATIONS	The characteristic of a clay when it is made up of separate layers, rather than a homogeneous mass.
LAYING UP	The process of rolling out sheets of clay on boards or in hollow moulds.
LEATHER-HARD	The state of dryness of clay prior to its becoming too hard to model.
MAGMA	Semi-molten rock from the interior of the earth.
MATURING TEMPERATURE	The temperature at which a glaze melts or a clay body reaches the point of optimum vitrification with no deformation of the form.
MODEL	A form used to determine the inner face of a mould and therefore that of the cast clay object.
MUFFLE	A lining inside a kiln which totally separates the forms to be fired from the burning fuel.
NATCH	A projection on one piece of a mould which coincides with a hollow on another piece of mould, to ensure proper registration when the mould is assembled.
PLASTICITY	The ability of the clay to retain its shape during forming and drying.
RAKU	A process, originating in Japan, of very rapid gloss firing.

A clay box in which objects are enclosed to protect them from direct contact with the flames of an open kiln.	SAGGAR
The scratching through one surface (slip or glaze) to reveal the colour of the surface underneath.	SGRAFFITO
The addition of excessive water upon a clay mass so that it loses its form and produces a muddy solution.	SLAKE
(1) Any solution of glaze materials and water. (2) A glaze which may be applied to greenware to produce a finished and glazed piece with one firing. (3) A glaze made from a clay which melts to form a glass.	SLIP GLAZE
A solution of clay and water which has a thick consistency.	SLURRY
Maintaining a steady temperature state in a kiln to produce an increase of heat work without an increase in temperature.	SOAK
A hardened steel chisel used for removing glaze and stilts from shelves and glazed objects.	SORTING TOOL
A preformed clay motif applied to a form to produce an image in relief.	SPRIG
A ceramic tripod upon which glazed ware is set in order to prevent the melting glaze from fixing the form to the kiln shelf during firing.	STILT
A material which retards the settling of solid materials in a solution.	SUSPENDER
The unit of measurement which describes the strength of a sodium silicate solution.	TWADDLE
The formation of a glass by melting.	VITRIFICATION
The process of preparing clay by hand prior to throwing.	WEDGE
The technique of partially immersing a clay form in an engobe to produce patches of colour.	WINDOW DIPPING

Further reading

Rhodes, D., *Clay and Glazes for the Potter*. New York, 1967.
Leach, Bernard, *A Potter's Book*. London, 1945; Levittown, NY, 1972.
Billington, D. M., *The Technique of Pottery*. London, 1962.
Charleston, R. J. (ed.), *World Ceramics: an illustrated history*. London, 1968.
Nordness, Lee (ed.), *Objects USA*. London and New York, 1970.
Haswell, J. M., *The Thames and Hudson Manual of Mosaic*. London, 1973; New York, 1974.

JOURNALS

Craft Horizons, bi-monthly.
Craft Review, monthly.

Index

tin, 144, 146, 148, 149
tin chloride, 144
tin glazes, 16, 17
titanium, 144, 148, 149; *see also* ilmenite, rutile
Toft, Thomas, *100*
tomb figures, 16
tools, forming, 47–52; cutting, 48, 49, *51*; turning, 50, 92; shaping, 50; texturing, 52; throwing, 82; for decorating, 101, 103, 104
topping up, 77
trailing, 107–8, 157
transfer, *152*, 168
· tridymite, 118
turning, 50, 81, 88, 92, *93*
twaddle, 75, 183

UNDERCUTS, 69, 72
under-glaze, 103, 104, 143
unpacking of kilns, 164–5
up-draught kilns, 37–8
uranium, 144, 148

USA, *19*, 20, 21, *74*, *79*, *151*, *191*

VACUUM, 94
vanadium pentoxide, 144, 148
vegetable matter, 117, 131
ventilation of kilns, 30, 32, 38, 116, 118, 162, 169
venturi jet, 38
vitrification, 26, 106, 118, 119, 154, 183
volcanic ash, 132
Voulkos, Peter, *19*
Vyse, Charles, *109*

WAD BOX, 56, 94, 95
warping, 60, 71, 75, 96, 114, 115
water, 21, 28, 75, 96; in throwing, 84, 91; in engobes, 106–7; in glazes, 127, 153
water and clay combinations, 24–5, *114*, 115
water (free), 24, 114, 116

wax resist, 103, 110–12, 154, 166
wax resist brushes, 101
wear on moulds, 76
weathering, 28
wedging 30, 31, 64, 81, *82*, *83*, 183
Wedgwood, 17, *18*
wheels, 13, 80, *81*, 87–9, 104, 123
wheel head, 85, 91
white earthenware, 17
whiting, *see* calcium carbonate
window dipping, 107, 183
wire tools, 48, 50, 91, 94
wood, 162
working properties of clay, 26–8; improving, 27, 28

YÜAN CERAMICS, *113*

ZINC, 129, 130–1, 132, 140, 141, 146, 148; glazes, 144, 148, 149
zirconium, 144, 148